A YANKEE CHRISTMAS

A YANKEE CHRISTMAS

Recipes, Crafts, and Carols

Introduction by Martha White

YANKEE BOOKS

CAMDEN · MAINE

Front jacket photograph by Ralph Copeland
Back jacket photograph © 1990 by Debbie Smith

Interior color photographs by Ralph Copeland
Food styling by Kristie T. Scott

Typeset by Typeworks, Belfast, Maine
Printed and bound by Worzalla, Stevens Point, Wisconsin

Library of Congress Cataloging-in-Publication Data
Burleigh, Russell
    A Yankee Christmas / Russell Burleigh, Carole Yeager, Cynthia Van
Hazinga
        p.   cm.
    ISBN 0-89909-316-7
    1. Christmas – United States.   2. Christmas cookery.   3. Christmas
music.   4. Christmas decorations – United States.   5. United States –
Social life and customs.   I. Yeager, Carole.   II. Van Hazinga,
Cynthia. III. Title.
GT4986.A1B87   1990
394.2'68282 – dc20   90-46637
                                                                        CIP

10 9 8 7 6 5 4 3 2 1

JACKET AND TEXT DESIGN BY LURELLE CHEVERIE, ROCKPORT, MAINE

Contents

Recipes
BY CYNTHIA VAN HAZINGA

CHRISTMAS CAKES

GIFTS FROM YOUR KITCHEN

Festive Holiday Loaves

Preserves, Relishes, and Chutneys

PICKLES

SPECIAL TREATS

SEASONAL LIBATIONS AND HOLIDAY DRINKS

FABULOUS HOLIDAY PARTIES

HOLIDAY OPEN HOUSE

Children's Christmas Party

Tree-Trimming Supper for the Neighbors

Carolers' Reward

Dessert Party

Victorian-Style Christmas Tea

FAMILY CHRISTMAS FEASTS

POLISH-AMERICAN CHRISTMAS EVE SUPPER

CHRISTMAS BRUNCH AT HOME

CHRISTMAS DINNER FOR THREE GENERATIONS

Crafts

BY CAROLE YEAGER

Carols

BY RUSSELL I. BURLEIGH

# ntroduction

In any conversation about New England Christmases and what constitutes the Yankee versions of old-fashioned, family fun, it's not long before the word *tradition* comes up. As I was considering this in thinking about this book, however, it occurred to me that I would be hard-put to pinpoint my own family traditions beyond the mere fact that we gather together. Some years we have had plum pudding all aflame, usually there is apple pudding pie, but the basic menu, and many other details of the holiday, change from year to year, depending on where we gather, and with whom, and for how long. One year all the Maine relatives in my family were misguided enough to gather before a dismally bedecked, indoor palm tree in Florida. The only thing white about that Christmas was our family name and the sand on the beach.

So, I was just beginning to feel bereft of serious family traditions – and a little forlorn at the thought that maybe I didn't have such a happy childhood as I thought I did – when I realized the funny connection between the words *tradition* and *treason*. Both stem from the Latin for *handing over* and it was here that I found my bearings. To many of us, traditions are the small, seasonal acts that it would be treason to do differently. For example, do you hang tinsel a strand at a time or toss great gobs of it at the tree? Perhaps you hang delicate glass icicles, instead. One way is tradition; any other way is treason and only you know the difference.

Suddenly, my traditions were popping up everywhere and some of them – or their opposites – may be familiar to you. As our family groupings change over the years, we are called upon to combine our various forms of celebration. The Christmas tree is often a telltale, causing even the most mild-mannered, Christmas humbugs to leap into the fray. Who cuts the tree and when should you bring it in – a week before, maybe the night before – and when must it go? Does your family gather to decorate it, with the children given full leeway, or is it a magical, Christmas morning surprise to delight young eyes? Perhaps you have an adults-only version, fully color-coordinated and symmetrical, with delicate glass and eggshell ornaments, and candles (and wet sponges ready) instead of electric lights.

There is a common moment of truth when newlyweds realize that his family always had a star on the treetop, while her side had an angel perched there. Christmas tree lights tend to elicit strong feelings, as well: small lights or big ones? one color or multi? blinking or constant? Will you string popcorn and cranberries, or make cookie ornaments? Do you add an ornament each year? Can you hang the delicate glass balls that have survived the many generations, or is this the year to defer to the new kitten that may climb (and topple) the tree, or the toddler who can be expected to do the same? Will you hang chocolate coins, or would the dog eat them? Is there an Advent calendar? What goes on the mantel or stairway?

The menu offers similar dilemmas, however delectable. Is it turkey or goose and do you serve it on Christmas Eve or Christmas day? Do you stuff it with chestnuts, or apples, or sausage? The choices are almost unlimited, but one is tradition, the other treason. Plum pudding or fruitcake? How many pies and of what fillings? Even if you agree on an apple pie, is it his aunt's recipe or your cousin's?

What is constant in all this, of course, is the spirit of celebration. As we form and reform our traditions, we define those that are important to us and choose among the many small gestures, or create new ones, looking for those that are most meaningful. Above all, Christmas is the time we gather with family and friends. As the days grow short and cold before the winter solstice, we bring in the greens of holly and mistletoe and fir, light the candles and lamps, and add light, fragrance, and warmth to our days. Gifts of summer jams speak of longer days, while gingerbread houses and freshly baked cookies add their scents to the air. We gather before the fire and are stirred to work with our hands – sewing or whittling or otherwise utilizing our often-neglected talents – to give of ourselves. The piano is opened, and the Christmas music is dug out from the piano bench. Carolers make their village rounds, we share hot cocoa or mulled cider, and exchange gifts.

The children write letters to Santa, hang stockings, and practice for the Christmas pageant, standing tall in their red plaids and black velvet. The well-worn Christmas books appear at bedtime, with the illustrations and the words we know by heart: " 'Twas the night before Christmas . . ."

This book in its three parts – the recipes and crafts and music of Christmas – gathers many traditions, from various origins, into one collection. It is meant to inspire your Christmas celebrations, adding to what you have culled from your own family traditions, and enriching your enjoyment of the holiday. The ideas are simple and homespun, more lavish with time and love than with materials. Instead of the glitter and gleam of the department store extravaganza, where Christmas starts the day after Thanksgiving, we offer a more homebound version where giving comes from within and we raise our voices, together, in celebration.

Martha White

B

RECIPES

The Foods and Feasts of a Traditional New England Christmas

Christmas is a time of feasting and parties, and yet it is not, in most of our minds and hearts, a time of experimentation or fashionable cuisine. What most of us want and expect at Christmastime is the traditional fare of the family we remember and the national or ethnic tradition to which we belong. For many Americans, from each of the fifty states, that means old-fashioned New England food. Others, including New Englanders, reach back further— to the countries of their immigrant ancestors. And yet for most of us, young families in particular, Christmas traditions are ones that develop and evolve, catch fire from those of friends and family members, grow deeper every year, and become beloved.

For all who celebrate Christmas, food is an important part of the holiday. It's a time of feasts with all the trimmings, a time of comfort and cheer at the darkest, coldest time of the year. Some of our most personal and emotional memories of childhood Christmases are centered on special holiday foods. Every family, every New England town and community, has its particular traditions, and many of them involve food and get-togethers of a particularly festive sort. This season of celebration, this bright and fragrant time of year, is linked closely to favorite foods and well-remembered repasts. Visions of sugarplums, memories of traditional cakes and cookies, gifts from the heart and hearth—these are what keep the spirit of Christmas alive from generation to generation.

It's surprising to remember that the first New Englanders, the Puritan colonists, did not celebrate Christmas at all. Keeping only the Sabbath as a holy day, they looked on Christmas, Easter, and all the saints' days as pagan and frivolous, superstitious, and profane. So, in fact, it was partly because of the continuing immigrant tradition, particularly perhaps the German, Dutch, and Scandinavian, as well as the secularization of society, that the American Christmas tradition was created. It caught on fast; by the early nineteenth century, expectations of joyful excess, traditions of giving, feasting, singing, and outpourings of spirit were the rule in both country and town. It is these Christmas traditions that we share with you here – both Yankee customs and ethnic ones – both to inspire and add to your family customs, and to draw on in creating contemporary celebrations which will delight your own family.

What is characteristically New England in a celebration of Christmas is, essentially, what is New England. It is a matter of outlook – of practicality and continuity; it is a matter of thriftiness and appreciation of nature's bounty from corn to cranberries; it is a matter of style – of closeness to the sea and the forest, seasoned with memories of homelands across the sea and with the traditions of hardworking ancestors. It is a respect for the past, and the value of things handmade, and an openness of mind to improving life. Certain annual Christmas rituals that are simple in themselves – getting the tree, baking cookies, stirring the pudding, going to church, singing carols, ringing bells, lighting candles, remembering friends – touch off strong feelings in all of us, joyous feelings that are larger than the acts themselves. Each of these small rituals may contribute to your own family's celebration and to making it one that satisfies you, year after year.

Around and among all these traditions is food – menus that combine Old World customs and New World ingredients, recipes that have been passed down for generations and shared among families, friends, or whole communities. Some of these recipes are collected here, along with suggested menus for festive family meals from several strong, New England, ethnic traditions, as well as ideas for both casual and more elaborate parties. There are recipes for gifts of food (some of them to be made well ahead of time), food meant to be wrapped and tied with ribbons, and all meant to be shared. There are recipes for special holiday libations, for cookies and cakes, and to include in a special party for children. Throughout, there is respect paid to practicality and the cook's convenience, but with the realization that it is, after all, Christmas.

And Christmas is a time for generosity, for largess, for lavishness of spirit. It's a time for irresistible foods, served up in style, and shared with those you love best.

Cynthia Van Hazinga

CHRISTMAS COOKIES

Almost everyone likes cookies and nothing is more Christmassy. Many of the classic varieties, which we think of as American and which have become traditional, were brought to these shores by German immigrants. The word itself comes from the Dutch, sure as Santa Claus, but in the last hundred years making cookies at Christmastime has become a significant part of a New England celebration and many New England churches hold "cookie walks" and sell cookies at their Christmas bazaars.

Baking an assortment of cookies for Christmas is not only traditional, it's great fun to do. For many Yankee cooks, it's an annual ritual. For some, the cookie bake goes on for weeks, but even if you have time for only one or two varieties, you know which are your favorites.

Cookies star at Christmas parties. Being invited to partake of a tray of assorted plain and fancy cookies is one of the most delightful Christmas experiences and one most of us recall from childhood. Children love to learn to bake cookies and enjoy instant success, for most cookies are simple to make. Wrapped neatly or boxed and mailed, a variety of cookies makes a wonderful gift.

The recipes that follow include family favorites, traditional cookies, and some upstarts that have caught on fast and are now becoming traditions.

Mildred Nelson's Sugar Cookies

Mildred Nelson, descended from one of the oldest families in Hillsborough, New Hampshire, ran a celebrated guest house called "The Parting Of the Ways," in Hillsborough Center during the 1930s and 1940s. Miss Nelson was a famous cook and her recipes have been handed down in the family. These are perfect sugar cookies, short, crisp, and delicious, designed to be cut into fancy Christmas shapes.

> 3 cups sifted flour
>
> 1½ cups sugar
>
> 1 teaspoon baking soda
>
> 2 teaspoons cream of tartar
>
> ¼ teaspoon salt
>
> 1 cup butter
>
> 2 large eggs
>
> 1 teaspoon vanilla

Sift dry ingredients together. Work in butter as for pastry. Add beaten eggs and vanilla. Roll very thin (on floured pastry cloth) and cut out into shapes.

Bake eight to ten minutes in a 350°F oven. Watch them closely; cookies should not brown. Remove from cookie sheets quickly and cool on racks.

Makes three dozen cookies.

Patty's Milanos

Patty Withington, who is Mildred Nelson's great-grand-niece and still lives next door to where the "ways part," has adapted the old family recipe with spectacular results. Patty's Milanos were acclaimed as "best of show" at a Christmas Cookie party near Hillsborough Center a few Christmases ago and everyone's been trying to get the recipe since then.

Bake one recipe of Mildred Nelson's Sugar Cookies. Then prepare the Chocolate Glaze:

10 ounces semi-sweet chocolate

3 tablespoons shortening

Melt chocolate and shortening in a double boiler. Cool slightly, then spread thinly on the rough sides of half the cookies, topping with the others, and set aside to cool.

Makes eighteen cookies.

Chocolate Oatmeal Cookies

Watch these closely as they bake – they burn easily. A crispy, delicious cookie. The grated orange peel is the secret ingredient.

6 ounces semi-sweet chocolate chips

½ cup butter

⅔ cup sugar

½ teaspoon almond extract

1 egg

1 cup flour

½ teaspoon baking soda

¼ teaspoon salt

1 cup oatmeal

1 cup coconut

1 tablespoon grated orange peel

Melt chocolate over hot water, cool.

Cream butter, sugar, almond extract. Beat in egg and melted chocolate.

Stir in flour, salt, and soda, then oatmeal, coconut, and

grated orange peel. Chill until dough can be easily handled.

Form into walnut-sized balls and flatten slightly on cookie sheets.

Bake ten to twelve minutes at 350°F. Remove from sheets carefully; these cookies harden as they cool.

Makes two dozen cookies.

Doris Fusco's Brown-Edged Sugar Cookies

This is an old recipe from western Vermont. The cookies are simple but delightful.

½ cup butter

1 cup sugar

1 beaten egg

⅔ cup milk

2½ cups flour

2 teaspoons cream of tartar

1 teaspoon baking soda

½ teaspoon salt

½ teaspoon lemon extract

1 teaspoon vanilla

Cream butter and sugar well. Add egg, beat well.

Add milk.

Sift flour with other dry ingredients. Add to creamed mixture. Then add lemon extract and vanilla.

Drop by rounded teaspoons on greased cookie sheet. Sprinkle with sugar and nutmeg. Put raisin or nut in center.

Bake at 350°F for ten to twelve minutes until brown
around the edges. Remove from sheets at once and
cool on rack.

Makes about three dozen cookies.

Aunt Jenny's Sugar Cookies

Aunt Jenny's cookies are easy to make and don't
need to be rolled out—just flatten each cookie with
a tumbler wrapped in a square of cloth or a dish
towel. The nuts are optional, but use them if you like
nuts. I think they make a good cookie even better.

½ cup butter

½ teaspoon salt

1 teaspoon vanilla

1 cup sugar (white or light brown)

2 eggs

2 cups flour

1 teaspoon baking powder

½ teaspoon soda

2 tablespoons milk

½ cup chopped nuts

Cream butter and sugar. Add salt, vanilla, and unbeaten
eggs, one at a time. Beat well.

Sift flour with baking powder and soda. Add to creamed
mixture.

Add milk and mix well, then add nuts.

Drop by spoonfuls onto cookie sheet and flatten each
cookie with the bottom of a glass covered with a
damp cloth.

Sprinkle with white or colored sugar.

Bake ten to twelve minutes in a 375°F oven.

Makes three dozen cookies.

Alyce King's Date Nut Cookies

"The longer you keep these the better they get," says
Alyce King of Benson, Vermont. They should be soft.
Mrs. King recommends putting a slice of bread into
the cookie jar to keep them that way.

1 cup sugar

1 egg

½ cup oil

½ cup molasses, mixed with ½ cup
water and 1 teaspoon soda

3½ cups flour

½ teaspoon salt

½ teaspoon cinnamon

½ teaspoon nutmeg

½ teaspoon cloves

½ cup chopped walnuts

½ cup chopped dates

Beat sugar with egg and oil. Add molasses mixture.

Sift dry ingredients together and add to molasses mixure.
Batter should be stiff.

Drop in teaspoonfuls onto lightly greased cookie sheets.

Bake twelve to fifteen minutes in a 350°F oven.

Makes four dozen cookies.

Best Toll House Cookies

It's possible that every man, woman, and child thinks their own mother made the best Chocolate Chip Cookies in the world. In my case, this is certainly true. This is how my mother made them at Christmastime. Because they have oatmeal in them, they stand up well to mailing and are good to tuck into stockings.

1½ cups flour

1 teaspoon baking soda

1 teaspoon salt

1 cup margarine or shortening

¾ cup brown sugar

¾ cup white sugar

2 unbeaten eggs

1 teaspoon hot water

1 cup chopped walnuts

1 cup chocolate chips

1 cup raisins

2 cups oatmeal

1 teaspoon vanilla

Sift flour, soda, and salt together in large bowl.

Cream shortening and sugars together.

Add eggs, one at a time, then teaspoon hot water, then flour mixture.

Fold in other ingredients.

Drop spoonfuls onto cookie sheets. Bake in 375°F oven for about eight minutes.

Makes about three dozen cookies.

Christmas Rum Balls

This recipe is a Christmas classic but not for the children. Make these cookies ahead of time to allow the flavors to develop. They can be varied with bourbon, Scotch whisky, or cointreau, and they are also delicious when chopped coconut is substituted for the chopped nuts. Pecans can be used instead of walnuts.

2 cups vanilla wafer crumbs

1 cup finely chopped walnuts

1 cup confectioners' sugar

2 tablespoons unsweetened cocoa

2 tablespoons light corn syrup

⅓ cup dark rum

Mix all ingredients well. (Walnuts are best chopped in a blender or food processor.) Chill dough.

Shape by teaspoonfuls into firm balls. Roll in confectioners' sugar or cocoa.

Store tightly covered or freeze.

Makes about four dozen.

Chocolate Pecan Wafers

These are crisp, thin chocolate cookies, each studded with a pecan half. A standby on the Christmas cookie tray; these may be my own very favorite cookies.

½ cup butter or margarine

¾ teaspoon salt

1 teaspoon vanilla

1 cup sugar

2 eggs

3 ounces melted unsweetened chocolate

¾ cup sifted flour

¾ cup chopped pecans

whole pecans to decorate

Combine butter or margarine, salt, and vanilla. Beat with
   sugar until light and fluffy.

Add eggs one at a time; blend in melted chocolate.

Add sifted flour and broken pecans.

Drop onto greased cookie sheet. Let stand a few minutes,
   then flatten each cookie with the bottom of a glass
   covered with a damp cloth. Place pecan half in
   center of each cookie.

Bake twelve minutes in 325°F oven.

Makes two and a half dozen cookies.

Chocolate Nut Bars

This is another classic cookie I remember from my
mother's cookie tray. These are toothsome.

½ cup butter

½ teaspoon almond extract

¾ cup confectioners' sugar

1 egg

2 ounces unsweetened chocolate

¾ cup chopped nuts

2 cups flour

½ teaspoon salt

additional confectioners' sugar

Cream butter, almond extract, and sugar.

Add egg, beat well.

Add melted chocolate; stir in nuts.

Mix well with flour and salt. Pack in a 6 x 10-inch pan,
   cover with waxed paper and chill at least one hour.

Cut into 3 x ¾-inch bars.

Bake in 375°F oven ten to twelve minutes.

Remove bars to rack and cool slightly, then roll in
   additional confectioners' sugar.

Makes two dozen bars.

Spicy Nut Triangles

A simple, crispy cookie that's spread in a pan rather
than rolled, so it's very easy to make. Delicious
with tea.

1 cup butter

1 cup sugar

1 egg, separated

2 cups sifted flour

½ teaspoon salt

1 teaspoon cinnamon

1 cup finely chopped walnuts

Cream butter and sugar well. Add egg yolk. Beat well.

Sift flour, salt, and cinnamon and mix in, stirring well.

Spread in 10 x 15-inch pan.

Beat egg white slightly. Brush over top.

Smooth surface with fingertip.

Sprinkle nuts over dough and press in.

Bake very slowly in 275°F oven about one hour.

While uncut cookie is still warm, cut into four lengthwise strips and then cut six crosswise strips. Cut again diagonally.

Makes four dozen cookies.

Ginger Crinkles

A solid, tasty ginger cookie that stands up well to packing and mailing. These are good cookies to leave out for Santa Claus – with a bottle of fresh milk.

> ¾ cup soft shortening or butter
>
> 1 cup sugar
>
> 1 egg
>
> ¼ cup molasses
>
> 2 cups sifted flour
>
> 2 teaspoons baking soda
>
> 1 teaspoon salt
>
> 1 teaspoon cinnamon
>
> ¾ teaspoon cloves
>
> ¾ teaspoon ginger

Cream shortening and sugar together, then add egg and molasses, and beat well.

Add dry ingredients and mix thoroughly.

Roll into balls the size of small walnuts and place about two inches apart on greased baking sheet.

Bake ten to twelve minutes in 375°F oven.

Remove from sheets and roll in granulated sugar while still warm.

Makes four to five dozen.

Chocolate Crinkles

These are a fitting companion to Ginger Crinkles. They look somewhat similar but taste very different. They are crisp cookies with a slightly chewy center.

> ½ cup margarine or butter
>
> 1⅔ cups sugar
>
> 2 teaspoons vanilla
>
> 2 eggs
>
> 2 ounces unsweetened chocolate, melted
>
> 2 cups sifted flour
>
> 2 teaspoons baking powder
>
> ½ teaspoon salt
>
> ½ cup milk
>
> 1 cup chopped walnuts

Cream butter or margarine with sugar and vanilla.

Beat in eggs, then chocolate.

Add sifted dry ingredients alternately with milk; mix thoroughly. Stir in nuts.

Chill mixture for two to three hours, then roll into balls one inch in diameter. Roll quite heavily in confectioners' sugar.

Bake on greased baking sheet, about two to three inches apart at 375°F for about fifteen minutes.

Makes three dozen.

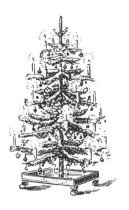

Molasses Filled Cookies

A very old-fashioned cookie that satisfies the eater in a basic, old-fashioned way. It's almost inconceivable to eat these without drinking a glass of cold milk.

> ½ cup butter or shortening
>
> ⅓ cup sugar
>
> 1 egg
>
> ⅔ cup dark molasses
>
> 2¾ cups sifted flour
>
> 1½ teaspoons baking powder
>
> ½ teaspoon salt
>
> 1 teaspoon ginger
>
> ½ teaspoon cinnamon
>
> 1 cup cookie filling or
>
> prepared mincemeat

Cream butter or shortening with sugar; add egg and molasses and beat well.

Sift together flour, baking powder, salt, and spices.

Add flour mixture to molasses mixture and combine.

Chill for about one hour.

Roll out to about one-eighth inch on floured pastry cloth. Cut into two-inch rounds or shapes with cookie cutter. On half the cookies, place about one rounded teaspoon filling, cover with the rest of the cookies. Press together gently; cut slashes on tops to about one-half inch from the sides.

Bake in 375°F oven for about ten minutes.

Makes about three dozen filled cookies.

Mildred Nelson's Fig or Raisin Cookie Filling

If Mildred Nelson made it, you know it's good. That hospitable woman had a sweet tooth that made her a particular favorite with the children in Hillsborough Center, New Hampshire.

> ½ pound figs, chopped fine
>
> (or chopped raisins)
>
> ⅓ cup sugar
>
> ⅓ cup boiling water
>
> 1 tablespoon lemon juice

Mix in order given and cook in double boiler until thick. Use to fill cookies.

Makes enough for two batches of molasses cookies.

Sissy Shattuck's Filled Cookies

Although Mrs. Shattuck came to New Hampshire from Austria, these are classic New England cookies. Years ago, cooks used a thimble to cut out the centers, making a ring-shaped cookie for the top.

For the cookies:

1 cup sugar

½ cup butter

1 egg

½ cup milk

1 teaspoon cream of tartar

½ teaspoon baking soda

about 2 cups flour, enough to make a
stiff dough that can be rolled out

Cream butter and sugar. Add egg, then a cup and a half
of the flour, cream of tartar, and soda. Roll out on
floured pastry cloth or board. Cut circles and rings
with cookie cutters.

Place circles on greased cookie sheet. Put one tablespoon
of filling in the center of each and top with a cookie
ring. Press the edges together with the tines of
a fork.

Bake in 375°F oven ten to twelve minutes. Cool on
wire rack.

For the filling:

⅔ cup raisins or part currants

½ cup water

½ cup sugar

2 teaspoons flour, moistened with
cold water

Cook together until thick (about ten minutes) over
medium heat, stirring frequently. After cooling, add
a little lemon extract.

Makes two and a half dozen cookies.

Saucepan Fruit Bars

A very Christmassy cookie, a little like a fruitcake.
Good frosted with Lemon Glaze. These cookies
keep well.

1 cup melted butter

1½ cups sugar

2 eggs

3 cups sifted flour

½ teaspoon baking soda

½ teaspoon salt

½ teaspoon ground nutmeg

½ teaspoon cloves

½ teaspoon cinnamon

½ cup sour cream

1 cup golden raisins

1 cup currants

1 cup chopped walnuts

Lemon Glaze

Mix 1 cup confectioners' sugar with ¼ teaspoon
lemon juice.

Melt butter in large saucepan. Add sugar and eggs and
beat well.

Add sifted dry ingredients and sour cream, then fold in
fruit and nuts.

Spread in greased 10 x 15-inch pan. Bake at 350°F
about twenty-five minutes. Brush with glaze; cool in
pan, then cut into bars.

Makes about two dozen.

Saucepan Brownies

My most efficient cousin, Christine Howe-Causar,
taught me how to make a batch of brownies in one
pan in ten minutes. It was a technique she developed
when her children were small. These are delicious.

> *3 ounces unsweetened chocolate*
>
> *⅓ cup butter*
>
> *1 cup sugar*
>
> *2 eggs*
>
> *¾ cup flour*
>
> *½ teaspoon baking powder*
>
> *½ teaspoon salt*
>
> *1 cup broken walnuts*

Using a good-quality saucepan, such as a copper-
bottomed stainless-steel pan, melt chocolate and
butter together over low heat.

Remove from heat and stir in sugar and eggs, using a
wire whisk. Beat well.

Sift flour, baking powder, and salt together straight into
the saucepan.

Stir in nuts, and pour batter into a greased, 8-inch
square pan.

Bake at 350°F about thirty minutes or less, so that
brownies are firm but fudgy.

Makes twelve to sixteen brownies.

Dublin Diamonds

These short, not-too-sweet cookies are cut into
diamond shapes and sparkle like diamonds with
sugar. Dublin, I think, is Dublin, New Hampshire.

> *2½ cups pastry flour*
>
> *1 teaspoon salt*
>
> *1 tablespoon sugar*
>
> *1½ teaspoons baking powder*
>
> *¼ cup butter*
>
> *½ cup raisins*
>
> *¼ cup currants*
>
> *¼ cup candied orange peel or citron,*
> *cut fine*
>
> *1 tablespoon caraway seed*
>
> *1 cup milk*
>
> *granulated sugar*

Sift together flour, salt, sugar, and baking powder.

Mix in butter with fingertips or pastry blender. Mix in
fruits and caraway seeds, then add milk.

Roll out one-half inch thick and cut into diamonds.
Sprinkle with granulated sugar.

Bake at 450°F for fifteen minutes.

Makes about two dozen.

Silvia's
Sunnyseed Cookies

A healthful honey and whole wheat cookie everyone
loves. This is the version from Silvia Spence.

1 cup oil

⅓ cup water

1⅓ cups honey

1 teaspoon vanilla

1 cup sunflower seeds

3 cups whole wheat flour

1 teaspoon baking powder

Mix together oil, water, and honey. Add vanilla.

Stir in dry ingredients.

Drop by spoonfuls onto greased or oiled cookie sheet.

Bake in 350°F oven for twelve to fifteen minutes or until
light brown.

Makes about three dozen.

Snowflake Cookies

Crispy, lacy-looking oatmeal cookies. Good to wrap
and give as gifts and a staple for the cookie plate on
the sideboard.

1½ cups oatmeal

1½ cups brown sugar

¼ cup flour

½ teaspoon salt

⅔ cup melted butter

1 egg

1 teaspoon vanilla

Mix oatmeal, brown sugar, flour, and salt.

Add melted butter, then slightly beaten egg, and vanilla.
Mix well.

Drop by teaspoonfuls about two inches apart on
ungreased cookie sheet.

Bake at 350°F about five minutes, until light brown.

Remove with a spatula to a rack. Cookies will firm up as
they cool.

Makes about four dozen.

Mary's Chewy Chocolate Cookies

Mary Howe-Gabrini is a wonderful Yankee cook
who makes the Christmas season special for many of
her friends. Every year, Mary bakes a variety of
cookies and gives them away in brightly wrapped
packages. People have begun to depend on her for
traditional treats. These cookies are exquisitely
chocolatey.

1¼ cups butter or margarine

2 cups sugar

2 eggs

1 teaspoon vanilla

2 cups flour

¾ cup unsweetened cocoa

1 teaspoon baking soda

½ teaspoon salt

1 cup chopped walnuts

1 cup chocolate chips

Cream butter and sugar; add eggs and vanilla, and
blend well.

Sift together dry ingredients, mix.

Stir in nuts and chocolate chips.

Drop by teaspoonfuls onto ungreased cookie sheets.

Bake at 350°F for eight to nine minutes. Do not
overbake.

Cool for about a minute on cookie sheet, then remove to wire rack to cool completely.

Makes about four dozen.

Mary's Snickerdoodles

Mary says she's been making these cookies since she was a child. For Christmas, she rolls them in red- and green-colored granulated sugar.

> ½ cup butter
>
> ½ cup shortening
>
> 1½ cups sugar
>
> 2 eggs
>
> 2¾ cups flour
>
> 2 teaspoons cream of tartar
>
> 1 teaspoon soda
>
> ½ cup colored sugars

Cream butter, shortening, sugar, and eggs.

Blend in dry ingredients. Chill.

Shape dough into small balls with hands.

Roll balls in colored sugar and place about two inches apart on ungreased cookie sheets.

Bake in 375°F oven eight to ten minutes or until set.

Makes about six dozen cookies.

Mary's Applesauce Cookies

These are very chewy and very good.

> 2 cups flour
>
> 1 teaspoon baking soda
>
> ½ teaspoon salt
>
> 1 teaspoon cinnamon
>
> 1 teaspoon nutmeg
>
> ½ teaspoon cloves
>
> ½ cup butter
>
> ½ cup brown sugar
>
> ½ cup white sugar
>
> 1 egg
>
> 1 cup smooth, thick applesauce
>
> 1 cup chopped raisins
>
> ½ cup chopped walnuts

Sift together dry ingredients.

Cream sugar and butter until light, stir in egg and applesauce.

Combine with flour mixture. Add raisins and nuts.

Drop by spoonfuls onto cookie sheets.

Bake at 425°F for eight to ten minutes or until lightly browned.

Makes about three dozen.

Walnut Thumbprint Cookies

Many people, including myself, zoom in on these cookies when they are spotted on a cookie tray at Christmastime.

1 cup butter

½ cup brown sugar

2 eggs, separated

1 teaspoon vanilla

2 cups flour

½ teaspoon salt

1½ cups finely chopped nuts

Mix butter, sugar, egg yolks, and vanilla.

Work in flour and salt until dough holds together. Chill.

Shape dough into small balls, about walnut-sized.

Dip each ball into slightly beaten egg white and roll in nuts.

Place about one inch apart on ungreased cookie sheet. Bake five minutes in a 375°F oven.

Press thumb deeply into center of each.

Bake about eight minutes longer or until light brown.

Remove from baking sheet and cool on wire rack. When cookies are cool, fill thumbprints with sparkling red or green jelly.

Makes four dozen.

Mary's Peanut Butter Cookies

This is another cookie Mary has been making all her life. No Christmas cookie selection is complete without them.

1 cup butter

1 cup good peanut butter

1 cup sugar

1 cup brown sugar

2 eggs

2½ cups flour

1½ teaspoons baking soda

1 teaspoon baking powder

½ teaspoon salt

Cream together butter, peanut butter, sugar, and eggs.

Blend in dry ingredients; cover and chill.

Form into one-inch balls and place three inches apart on lightly greased baking sheet.

With fork, flatten cookies in criss-cross pattern to about two inches.

Bake in 350°F oven for ten to twelve minutes until set but not hard.

Makes about six dozen cookies.

Mary's Nut Butter Cookies

These are pure buttery delight. Cut in small circles, they are sandwiched in pairs with raspberry jam and the tops are dusted with confectioners' sugar.

1 cup butter

2 cups flour

½ cup sugar

1 teaspoon vanilla

1 cup very finely chopped walnuts

raspberry jam

confectioners' sugar

Mix first five ingredients and chill.

Roll out dough on pastry cloth about one-quarter inch
thick and cut into one and one-half-inch circles.

Bake on ungreased cookie sheets about ten to twelve
minutes at 350°F. Do not brown.

Cool, then sandwich in pairs with jam; sprinkle
with sugar.

Makes about two dozen cookies.

Aunt Amy's Cornmeal Cookies

A simple, unusual cookie. The cornmeal makes them
delightfully crunchy.

¾ cup butter

¾ cup sugar

1 egg

1½ cups flour

1 teaspoon baking powder

¼ teaspoon salt

½ cup cornmeal

½ teaspoon nutmeg

½ cup raisins

½ cup chopped walnuts

Cream butter and sugar.

Add egg and beat well, then add the rest of the
ingredients.

Drop by spoonfuls on a greased cookie sheet.

Bake at 350°F for twelve to fifteen minutes.

Makes three dozen cookies.

Mildred Nelson's Coconut Date Cookies

A favorite of Hillsborough Center children. Mildred
Nelson's grand-niece gave me this old-fashioned,
time-honored family recipe. If you like, place a
candied cherry in the center of each.

1 egg

⅓ cup shortening

¾ cup sugar

⅓ cup dates

⅓ cup shredded coconut

⅓ cup walnuts

⅜ cup milk

1 teaspoon lemon extract

2 cups flour

3 teaspoons baking powder

½ teaspoon salt

candied cherries (optional)

Beat together the egg, shortening, and sugar until light-
colored and creamy.

Add fruits and then dry ingredients alternately with milk
and lemon extract, stirring just enough to combine.

Drop by spoonfuls onto baking sheet.

Bake in 375°F oven for ten to twelve minutes or until just done. Cool on wire rack.

Makes about three dozen cookies.

Cranberry Oatmeal Christmas Cookies

This recipe makes a big batch of fresh-tasting, crunchy cookies. A good bet to send to school for a classroom party, or to keep in a jar for young visitors. Use part whole wheat flour for extra crunch.

> 2 cups cranberries
>
> 1 cup granulated sugar
>
> 1 cup butter or margarine
>
> 1¼ cups brown sugar
>
> 2 eggs
>
> 1½ cups flour (or use part
>   whole wheat flour)
>
> ½ teaspoon salt
>
> 1 teaspoon baking powder
>
> 1 teaspoon baking soda
>
> 1 teaspoon vanilla
>
> ½ cup buttermilk
>
> 1 tablespoon grated orange peel
>
> 2 cups oatmeal
>
> 1 cup chopped walnuts

Chop cranberries coarsely. (The best way to do this is with a curved knife in a wooden bowl or with a food processor.)

Combine cranberries with one-half cup of the granulated sugar and set aside.

Cream the rest of the sugars with butter or margarine and then beat in eggs. Add vanilla.

Sift dry ingredients together and add to creamed mixture alternately with splashes of buttermilk.

Mix in oatmeal, orange peel, and nuts, then fold in cranberries.

Drop by tablespoons onto greased cookie sheet about two inches apart.

Bake in 375°F oven for ten to twelve minutes until lightly browned and almost firm. Cool on wire racks.

Makes about five dozen cookies.

Brown-Edged Chunky Cookies

These cookies are very popular with children. The chunks are chocolate, walnuts, coconut, oatmeal, and raisins. These cookies have a very good flavor.

> 2½ cups flour
>
> 2 teaspoons baking powder
>
> ½ teaspoon salt
>
> 1 cup butter
>
> ¾ cup brown sugar
>
> ½ cup corn syrup
>
> 2 eggs
>
> 1 teaspoon vanilla
>
> ¼ cup milk
>
> 1 cup chocolate chips
>
> 1 cup oatmeal
>
> 1 cup coconut
>
> 1 cup walnut pieces
>
> 1 cup raisins

Sift flour, baking powder, and salt and set aside.

Cream butter with sugar, then beat in corn syrup, mixing well. Add eggs one at a time, beating well after each addition.

Add vanilla, then dry ingredients alternately with milk. Mix well. Add oatmeal and coconut.

Fold in chocolate, nuts, and raisins.

Chill dough about one-half to one hour.

Drop by rounded teaspoons onto cookie sheets.

Bake in 375°F oven twelve to fifteen minutes.

Cool on racks.

Makes about four dozen cookies.

Butter Brickle Cookies

These are sinfully good. Heath's Bits 'o Brickle are hard to find except at Christmastime, and they are the raison d'etre of these special, sweet cookies. These pack and ship well.

> 1 six-ounce package Heath's Bits 'o Brickle almond chips
>
> 2 tablespoons melted butter
>
> ¼ cup flour
>
> ½ cup butter
>
> ⅓ cup sugar
>
> ⅓ cup brown sugar
>
> 1 teaspoon vanilla
>
> 2 eggs
>
> ½ teaspoon salt
>
> ½ teaspoon baking soda
>
> 1½ cups flour

Toss brickle bits with melted butter and then one-quarter cup flour. Set aside.

Cream butter and sugars, add vanilla. Beat well. Add eggs one at a time and beat well.

Add dry ingredients gradually. Mix. Add floured brickle chips and mix.

Roll teaspoonfuls of cookie dough into small balls, each about the size of a walnut, and bake at 325°F for about twelve minutes or until golden brown.

Remove from cookie sheets and cool on racks.

Makes about four dozen cookies.

Chinese Chews

Who knows why these cookies were ever called "Chinese"? Anyway, they are classic Yankee cookies.

> ¾ cup flour
>
> ¼ teaspoon salt
>
> 1 teaspoon baking powder
>
> 1 cup sugar
>
> 1 cup chopped dates
>
> 1 cup chopped nuts
>
> 3 eggs

Sift dry ingredients together.

Beat eggs well.

Stir remaining ingredients into flour mixture.

Spread in 10 x 14-inch pan.

Bake in 300°F oven thirty minutes.

Cut into bar cookies.

Makes about three dozen cookies.

Miss Pearl Ray's Pineapple Cookies

The late Pearl Ray, a wonderful woman in the traditional Yankee mold, lived most of her life with her brother in the house where her parents and grandparents had lived before her. The Rays were a fixture in Hillsborough's Concord End, and their farm a reminder of days mostly passed. Pearl Ray pumped water and cooked on a woodstove, and these are her cookies.

> 1 scant cup sugar
>
> ½ cup shortening
>
> 1 egg
>
> ½ cup crushed drained pineapple
>
> ¼ teaspoon soda
>
> 1 teaspoon baking powder
>
> ⅛ teaspoon salt
>
> 2 cups flour, sifted before measuring

Cream together sugar and shortening.

Add egg, beat well.

Add pineapple, soda, baking powder, salt, and flour.

Drop from teaspoon onto greased cookie sheet.

Bake at 375°F about eight to ten minutes.

Makes three dozen cookies.

CHRISTMAS CAKES

Many New England cooks bake a certain cake that means Christmas in that family. It's usually fruity, but today's cook is likely to concoct a lighter cake than our grandmothers did. Any of these cakes could serve as the pièce de resistance at a holiday buffet or to top off a family celebration dinner.

Pecan Cake

This small fruitcake is simple to make and yet very delicious. Serve it to guests with eggnog or coffee, or top with ice cream or whipped cream for a festive dessert. Grating the nutmeg fresh makes a big difference. You may need to cook it a little longer; test it — a toothpick should come out clean when it's done. It keeps well if tightly covered and will stay moist if you give it an occasional shower of brandy.

½ cup butter or margarine

1 cup sugar

3 whole eggs

1 cup sifted flour

½ teaspoon fresh grated nutmeg

½ teaspoon cinnamon

½ teaspoon baking powder

pinch of salt

2 ounces brandy

1 cup raisins

1 cup coconut

2 cups pecan halves or pieces

Set raisins aside to macerate in brandy. Cream butter and sugar until light and fluffy. Add eggs one at a time and beat well. Sift flour with dry ingredients and add to the egg mixture. Stir in the fruit and nuts. Turn into a well-greased 9-inch tube pan.

Bake at 350°F for about one and one-quarter hours.

Makes one cake.

Easy Applesauce Spice Cake

This is a small, simple, spicy cake. Use either raisins or currants; at Christmastime I prefer currants. This cake keeps well.

½ cup butter or margarine

½ cup sugar

2 eggs

½ cup molasses

2 cups all-purpose flour

1 teaspoon baking powder

½ teaspoon baking soda

¼ teaspoon salt

1 teaspoon cinnamon

½ teaspoon nutmeg

¼ teaspoon ground cloves

1 cup thick applesauce

1 cup cut raisins or currants

Cream shortening and sugar and add eggs, then molasses, beating well.

Sift dry ingredients together and add alternately with applesauce. Fold in currants or raisins.

Bake in greased 9-inch square pan in a moderate oven (350°F) for about forty-five minutes or until center tests done with a toothpick.

Makes one cake.

Mincemeat Fruit Cake

This is a well-used recipe from Alyce King's family, well known in western Vermont. "Make it before Thanksgiving," she says. "I've made it myself hundreds of times."

9 ounces mincemeat

1½ cups water

2½ cups flour

1 teaspoon baking soda

2 beaten eggs

15 ounces condensed milk

2 cups mixed candied fruits

1 cup nuts

1 cup chopped dates

1 cup chopped figs

Cook mincemeat in water; cool. Add beaten eggs.

Mix in sifted dry ingredients, fruits, and nuts, alternately with additions of milk. Batter will be stiff.

Bake at 350°F for about forty-five minutes.

Makes two loaves.

Mother's Fruit Cake

"Very nice and will keep well," says the notation in Mother's old-fashioned script. (This is not my mother's but Mildred Nelson's.)

> 1 cup butter
>
> 2 cups sugar
>
> 5 eggs
>
> 4 cups flour
>
> 1 teaspoon baking soda
>
> 1 teaspoon cinnamon
>
> ½ teaspoon nutmeg
>
> ½ teaspoon mace
>
> ½ teaspoon ground cloves
>
> ½ teaspoon allspice
>
> ⅔ cup milk
>
> 1 pound raisins
>
> ½ pound currants
>
> ¼ pound citron

Cream butter and sugar. Add eggs and beat well.

Sift flour and stir together flour and spices. Add gradually to creamed mixture, alternately with milk, mixing together carefully.

Fold in fruits.

Bake in buttered 9-inch tube pan in a 350°F oven for about one hour or more. Test with straw or wooden pick to be sure it is done.

Wrap well and put away for Christmas.

Makes one cake.

Chocolate Fruit Cake

This is a very easy fruitcake from an old New England recipe. It's small and rich. This is the solution for a family in which some think all cakes should be chocolate.

> ½ cup butter
>
> 1 cup sugar
>
> ¼ cup cocoa powder
>
> 3 egg yolks
>
> ½ cup water
>
> 1 teaspoon vanilla
>
> 1¼ cups flour
>
> 1 teaspoon baking powder
>
> 1 teaspoon cinnamon
>
> 3 egg whites, beaten stiff
>
> ½ cup candied cherries
>
> ½ cup golden raisins
>
> ½ cup chopped walnuts

Cream butter and sugar, then mix in cocoa, eggs, and vanilla. Beat well.

Add sifted dry ingredients alternately with water.

Finally, fold in egg whites, fruit, and nuts. Spoon into 8- or 9-inch tube pan, well buttered, and lined with waxed paper.

Bake at 325°F for about one hour or until cake tests done.

Cool and frost with Chocolate Glaze. Decorate with candied cherry halves and walnuts.

Makes one cake.

Chocolate Glaze

This is shiny and dramatic. It's perfect for a Christmas cake decorated with cherries and silver shot.

> 4 ounces unsweetened chocolate
>
> ⅔ cup chocolate chips
>
> 8 ounces butter
>
> 2 tablespoons corn syrup

Melt the chocolates in a double-boiler, then beat in the butter one tablespoon at a time. Mix in the corn syrup and then cool—keep an eye on it and stir frequently—until it is of spreading consistency.

Chocolate Date Cake

Another favorite for that family which insists on chocolate everything. This is a moist, inexpensive, chocolate cake made with cocoa and buttermilk. The chopped dates make it extra special. At Christmastime I bake it in a tree-shaped pan; any pan with dimensions about 7 x 11 inches works well.

> ½ cup butter
>
> 1 cup sugar
>
> 2 eggs
>
> ½ cup unsweetened cocoa
>
> 1 cup flour
>
> ¾ teaspoon baking soda
>
> ¾ teaspoon baking powder
>
> ¼ teaspoon salt
>
> 1 cup buttermilk
>
> 1 cup chopped dates

Cream butter and sugar until light; beat in eggs one at a time.

Sift dry ingredients together.

Add to batter alternately with buttermilk, mixing only to blend.

Fold in chopped dates.

Bake in shaped pan or rectangle about 7 x 11 inches at 350°F for about forty-five minutes.

Frost with chocolate butter cream.

Makes one cake.

Sylvia's Pumpkin Cake

A moist, spicy cake just the way my mother used to make it. The addition of cherries makes it especially festive.

> 2 cups sugar
>
> 2 cups pumpkin puree
>
> 4 eggs
>
> 1¼ cups cooking oil
>
> 3 teaspoons cinnamon
>
> 1 teaspoon salt
>
> 1 teaspoon baking soda
>
> 1 tablespoon baking powder
>
> 3 cups flour
>
> about 10 candied cherries, chopped
>
> ¾ cup raisins
>
> ½ cup nuts

Mix together sugar, pumpkin, and eggs. Beat well.

Add oil.

Stir in dry ingredients, sifted together.

Fold in fruit and nuts.

Pour into greased, 9-inch tube pan or large loaf pan.

Bake forty-five to fifty minutes in a 350°F oven.

Serves eight to ten.

White Christmas Cake

A delicate, silvery white layer cake with coconut filling and fluffy white frosting, this can be decorated with more coconut and silver dragees, or candied cherries in a ring.

For the cake:

¾ cup butter

2 cups sugar

2 cups cake flour

2 teaspoons baking powder

¼ teaspoon salt

½ cup milk

8 egg whites

1 teaspoon almond extract

Cream butter and add sugar very gradually, beating after each addition until well blended.

Sift dry ingredients together. Add alternately to creamed mixture with milk. Add almond flavoring. Beat well.

Beat egg whites until stiff. Cut and fold them into the batter.

Pour into well-buttered, 8-inch cake pans.

Bake in 350°F oven twenty to twenty-five minutes or until done.

Cool in pans ten minutes and then cool completely before frosting.

For the filling:

2 tablespoons cornstarch

1 cup confectioners' sugar

2 egg yolks

1 cup milk

1 tablespoon butter

juice and rind of one lemon

1 cup flaked coconut

Mix cornstarch, sugar, and egg yolks, then add milk and butter and cook for about twenty minutes in a double boiler or heavy saucepan, stirring frequently.

When mixture is thickened and smooth, stir in lemon juice, grated rind, and coconut. Cool before spreading between layers of cake.

For the frosting:

2 egg whites

1½ cups sugar

⅓ cup cold water

¼ teaspoon cream of tartar

dash of salt

½ teaspoon lemon extract

1 teaspoon lemon zest

Place egg whites, sugar, water, cream of tartar, and salt in top of double boiler and mix.

Cook over hot water, beating constantly until mixture stands in peaks, about seven minutes. Remove from heat.

Add lemon extract and lemon zest. Beat until of spreading consistency.

Makes one cake.

Rhubarb Cake

Anyone who grows rhubarb can be counted on to have plenty of packages of it, chopped and frozen, left by Christmas. Otherwise, you may find it in the frozen food section of your supermarket. Next year, remember to pick it young and pink. This simple cake has a streusel topping and benefits by a drift of whipped cream on each portion.

For the cake:

½ cup butter or margarine

¾ cup brown sugar

½ cup white sugar

1 egg

2 cups flour

1 teaspoon baking soda

½ teaspoon salt

1 cup buttermilk

1 teaspoon vanilla

1½ cups diced fresh or frozen rhubarb

Cream butter or margarine with sugars until light and
fluffy.

Add egg; beat well. Add vanilla.

Sift dry ingredients together.

Add dry ingredients alternately with buttermilk.

Fold in rhubarb.

Spoon into 10-inch cake pan at least two inches deep.

For the topping:

½ cup brown sugar

1 teaspoon cinnamon

½ cup chopped nuts

Mix ingredients for topping and sprinkle evenly over
cake.

Bake in 350°F oven for about forty-five minutes or until
wooden pick inserted in center comes out dry.

Makes one 10-inch cake; serves six to eight.

Blueberry Gingerbread

This is moist and delectable. Serve warm with whipped cream or cold with vanilla ice cream. This is an old New Hampshire recipe.

½ cup butter

1 cup sugar

1 cup molasses

2 eggs

2½ cups flour

1 teaspoon ginger

1 teaspoon cinnamon

½ teaspoon cloves

½ teaspoon salt

1 teaspoon baking soda

¾ cup boiling water

1 cup frozen or fresh blueberries

Mix butter, sugar, and molasses. Add eggs.

Sift dry ingredients twice.

Add to first mixture. Mix.

Add boiling water and mix again.

Fold in blueberries last.

Bake in 12 x 18-inch pan in 350°F oven for about
thirty-five minutes or until done.

Serves twelve.

Blueberry Pudding Cake

A four-star winner at our family's supper table. This is really a simple blueberry cobbler that turns a late-winter supper into a celebration.

> ½ cup sugar
>
> 1 tablespoon cornstarch
>
> ¾ cup water
>
> 1 teaspoon grated lemon peel
>
> 2 cups frozen (or fresh) blueberries
>
> 1½ cups flour
>
> 3 teaspoons baking powder
>
> ¼ teaspoon salt
>
> ½ teaspoon cinnamon
>
> ½ cup butter or margarine
>
> ¾ cup sugar
>
> ½ cup milk

Make blueberry sauce by combining lemon peel, sugar mixed with cornstarch, and water in a saucepan. Cook, stirring constantly, just until mixture comes to a boil, then boil one minute. Remove from heat; add berries. Pour into an 8-inch square or round pan.

Sift dry ingredients together and set aside.

Cream butter or margarine and sugar until light. Add dry ingredients alternately with milk and beat until smooth.

Spread batter evenly over blueberry sauce.

Bake in 375°F oven thirty-five to forty minutes or until top is golden brown.

Serve with whipped cream or vanilla ice cream.

Makes eight portions.

Pumpkin Cheesecake

This has a light, spicy pumpkin flavor and a dense, creamy texture. If you have frozen pumpkin puree in your freezer, it will be especially flavorful.

> 2 pounds cream cheese
>
> 1 cup sugar
>
> 6 eggs
>
> 1½ cups concentrated pumpkin puree
>
> ¼ cup flour
>
> ½ teaspoon ginger
>
> ½ teaspoon nutmeg
>
> ½ teaspoon cloves
>
> ½ teaspoon allspice

Cream cream cheese well, add sugar, and beat until fluffy.

Add eggs one at a time, then pumpkin.

Mix in flour and spices and pour into 9-inch springform pan lined with graham cracker crust. Make sure your springform pan is watertight and set it in another pan (a roasting pan works well), filled with one inch of water.

Bake slowly at 300°F in water bath for at least one hour, then allow to sit in oven with heat turned off for another half hour.

Cool, then chill. Garnish with a ring of whipped cream sprinkled with chopped walnuts.

Serves ten to twelve.

Cranberry Cheesecake

I am delighted with this cake, which combines sweet, creamy cheesecake and the tart-sweet flavor of cranberries. It's a beautiful cake, and nothing is more suitable for Christmastime. This recipe calls for a crust of graham cracker crumbs; you might substitute gingersnaps. If you do, omit the cinnamon.

> ½ cup butter
>
> 1½ cups graham cracker crumbs
>
> ½ teaspoon cinnamon
>
> 2 tablespoons sugar
>
> 2 pounds cream cheese
>
> 1 cup sugar
>
> 2 tablespoons cornstarch
>
> 1 tablespoon grated lemon rind
>
> juice of one lemon
>
> 4 eggs
>
> 2 teaspoons vanilla
>
> 1 cup sour cream
>
> 2 cups jellied cranberry sauce

For the crust:

Melt butter. Mix with crumbs, sugar, and cinnamon.

Press the mixture on the sides and bottom of a 9-inch springform pan.

Bake in 350°F oven for ten minutes.

Remove and set aside to cool.

For the cheesecake:

Mix all remaining ingredients except cranberry sauce until blended smoothly. (I always do this in batches in a blender; a food processor or a mixing bowl works equally well. If you use a blender or food processor, pour the mixture into a bowl.)

Remove one-half cup of the mixture and pour the rest into the crumb crust. Blend the reserved batter with the jellied cranberry sauce until smooth.

Then pour a ring of the bright, cranberry-colored batter into the rest of the batter and stir with a knife to marbelize it.

Bake in 325°F oven with a pan of water on the bottom shelf for one and one-half hours. Turn off oven and let cake cool in oven. (This prevents cracking.)

Refrigerate before serving.

For the topping:

> 1½ cups sour cream
>
> 4 tablespoons sugar
>
> 1 teaspoon vanilla

Blend all ingredients together.

Spread over cooled cake.

Refrigerate for at least four hours before serving.

Serves ten to twelve.

Old-Fashioned Pound Cake with Currants

Sultanas may be substituted for currants in this high, fine-textured pound cake, a traditional New England holiday favorite.

> 2½ cups flour
>
> 2 teaspoons baking powder
>
> 1 teaspoon salt
>
> ½ teaspoon mace
>
> 1½ cups currants
>
> ¾ cup butter
>
> 1½ cups sugar
>
> 3 eggs
>
> 1 cup milk

Sift flour with baking powder, salt, and mace. Toss currants with one-half cup of the mixture and set aside.

Cream butter and sugar until light and fluffy.

Add eggs one at a time. Beat well.

Add dry ingredients alternately with milk, blending thoroughly. Begin and end with dry ingredients.

Fold in floured currants.

Bake in well-buttered, 10-inch tube pan in 325°F oven for one to one and one-quarter hours.

Serves eight to ten.

Gifts From Your Kitchen

Most cooks love to treat family and friends to a taste of what's been cooking, and everyone loves a homemade gift. Cooking or baking something intended for someone beloved is a special pleasure, and the real gift is love. Here are some traditional New England recipes that keep or travel well and say Merry Christmas when they arrive.

FESTIVE HOLIDAY LOAVES

Spicy Apple Loaf

In cool storage, New England apples keep well until Christmastime. Use any variety of crisp apple such as Cortland or Baldwin, even Yellow Delicious or Macintosh. This is my own recipe for a simple, delicious quick bread. It's flavorful, not too sweet, and easy to slice, perfect to accompany coffee or tea, perfect to give as a gift. Keep the extra loaf on hand to serve when unexpected guests drop by.

> 3 eggs
>
> 1½ cups sugar
>
> 1 cup butter or margarine, melted
>> and cooled
>
> 3 cups sifted, all-purpose flour
>
> 1½ teaspoons baking soda
>
> ½ teaspoon salt
>
> 1 teaspoon cinnamon
>
> ½ teaspoon each of nutmeg, allspice,
>> and ground cloves
>
> ⅔ cup buttermilk
>
> 2 cups grated apples (about two)
>
> 1 cup chopped walnuts

Preheat oven to 325°F and butter two 8½ x 4½-inch loaf pans. Line the bottoms with waxed paper.

Beat eggs with sugar. Add melted butter or margarine, then the sifted dry ingredients alternately with the buttermilk.

Fold in grated apple and walnuts.

Spoon into prepared pans and bake for about one hour. Test centers of loaves with a toothpick; if it comes out clean and the loaves are brown, they are done.

Makes two loaves.

Pineapple Pecan Loaf

This delicious, sweet quick bread is good plain, or toasted and spread with butter or cream cheese.

> ¾ cup brown sugar
>
> ½ cup butter
>
> 1 egg
>
> 2 cups flour
>
> 1 teaspoon baking soda
>
> ¼ teaspoon salt
>
> ⅓ cup fresh orange juice
>
> 1 eight-ounce can crushed pineapple
>
> 1 cup chopped pecans
>
> 2 tablespoons grated orange rind

Cream sugar and butter; add egg and beat well.

Sift flour before measuring. Sift again with dry ingredients. Add alternately with orange juice, mixing just to moisten.

Fold in undrained pineapple, pecans, and orange rind.

Pour into well-greased 8½ x 4½-inch loaf pan.

Bake in 350°F oven for about one hour.

Cool before wrapping.

Makes one loaf.

Mary's Fresh Fruit Bread

Mary Howe-Gabrini gave me the recipe for this fresh-tasting, holiday quick bread, with the guarantee, "It's delicious–" It can be served with whipped cream for a dessert or with cream cheese for a party sandwich. Its quick preparation depends on using a blender and it keeps well for at least a week.

½ cup fresh orange juice

2 eggs

½ cup soft shortening

1⅓ cups sugar

1½ cored, sliced apples

1 seeded orange, including peel

1 cup raisins

½ cup nuts

3 cups flour

1 teaspoon baking soda

1½ teaspoons baking powder

1 teaspoon salt

Assemble in a blender: orange juice, eggs, shortening, and sugar. Blend well.

Add orange and apples to the blender and blend until fruit is chopped fine.

Add raisins and nuts and blend fifteen seconds.

Add to sifted dry ingredients and stir to mix. Bake in greased and floured 9½ x 5½-inch loaf pan in 350°F oven about one and one-quarter hours or until it tests done.

Makes one large loaf.

Cranberry Walnut Loaf

The inclusion of coconut takes this quick bread out of the realm of the ordinary.

2½ cups flour

3 teaspoons baking powder

½ teaspoon salt

¾ cup butter or margarine

1½ cups sugar

3 eggs

2 teaspoons vanilla

⅔ cup orange juice

2 cups roughly chopped cranberries

1 cup chopped walnuts

1 cup coconut

2 tablespoons grated orange rind

Sift dry ingredients together and set aside.

Cream butter or margarine and sugar. Add eggs and beat well. Add vanilla.

Add dry ingredients alternately with orange juice, mixing just enough to moisten. Gently add cranberries, nuts, coconut, and grated peel.

Pour into two greased 8 x 3¾-inch loaf pans, and bake in 350°F oven, one and one-quarter hours, or until middle tests done.

Cool in pans, then finish cooling on wire rack.

When completely cool, wrap in plastic or foil.

Well-wrapped, this bread keeps two weeks in refrigerator or breadbox. Freezes well.

Makes two loaves.

Best Zucchini Bread

Rare indeed is the Yankee cook who hasn't cached plenty of grated, drained zucchini in the freezer. If you didn't freeze grated zucchini this year, make a note to do it next fall. Anyone who's tired of zucchini in September will be ready again by Christmas. This recipe was given to me by a friend in western Massachusetts and it's the best I've ever tried.

> 3 eggs
>
> 1 cup salad oil
>
> 2 cups peeled, coarsely grated zucchini
>
> 2½ cups sugar (or substitute
>
>   1 cup molasses)
>
> 1½ teaspoons vanilla
>
> 3 cups flour
>
> 1 teaspoon salt
>
> 1 teaspoon cinnamon
>
> ½ teaspoon cloves
>
> 1 teaspoon baking soda
>
> 1½ teaspoons baking powder
>
> 1 cup chopped nuts

Beat eggs well. Add oil and sugar, then zucchini and
    vanilla.

Sift dry ingredients together and add to zucchini mixture.

Fold in chopped nuts.

Pour into two greased and floured loaf pans or one
    10-inch bundt pan.

Bake in a 350°F oven for about one hour. Test with
    toothpick to be sure it is done.

Makes one large cake or two loaves.

Anadama Bread

A loaf of fresh, homemade bread is a welcome gift at Christmastime, and Anadama, with its fragrant molasses smell, is perhaps the most homespun of the native New England breads.

> 2 cups milk
>
> ½ cup water
>
> ½ cup yellow cornmeal
>
> ¼ cup butter
>
> ½ cup molasses
>
> 2 teaspoons salt
>
> 2 packages dry yeast or 2 tablespoons
>
>   active yeast
>
> 5 to 6 cups flour

Bring milk, water, and cornmeal to a boil.

Remove from heat. Add butter, molasses, and salt and
    cool to lukewarm.

Add yeast and stir to dissolve.

Add flour to make a fairly stiff dough. Knead well.

Place in greased bowl and let rise in a warm place until
    doubled in size.

Punch down, shape into two loaves, let rise again.

Bake in 350°F oven for about forty-five to fifty minutes
    or until done.

Makes two loaves.

Preserves, Relishes, and Chutneys

Cranberry and Quince Preserves

Popular-again quinces are an old New England standby. This is delicious on toast or plain cake or even with vanilla ice cream.

> 3 cups fresh or frozen cranberries
>
> 2 cups peeled chopped quinces
>
> 2 cups peeled chopped apples
>
> ¼ cup orange juice
>
> grated rind of 1 orange
>
> 4 cups sugar

Combine all ingredients in an enamel or stainless-steel kettle and cook slowly together until thick, stirring frequently to prevent sticking and burning. Cooking time is approximately one to one and a half hours.

Ginger Pear Chutney

This chutney is a favorite of mine and my friends. It turns a simple rice and curry dinner into an exotic feast. There's a certain neighborhood pear tree that usually provides fruit for my pear chutney, just as it did for my mother when she used to can pears. I make a really hot chutney; add chili peppers to your own taste.

> 4 quarts peeled, roughly chopped pears
>
> 3 large onions, chopped
>
> 3 large red peppers, chopped
>
> 3 cloves garlic, minced
>
> 2 cups sultanas
>
> 3 cups brown sugar
>
> 4 cups vinegar
>
> 2 tablespoons mustard seed
>
> 4 inches fresh ginger root, grated
>
> 2 teaspoons salt
>
> hot peppers to taste (at least one)

Combine all ingredients in a large stainless-steel or enamel kettle and cook slowly until thickened, about one hour, stirring often, watching carefully to see that it does not stick and burn. Pour, boiling hot, into sterile jars and seal.

Makes about five pints.

Apple Butter

Spicy apple butter, a New England classic, is cooked in fresh, sweet apple cider so that it requires relatively little sugar to sweeten and thicken it.

> 6 pounds tart cooking apples
>
> 2 cups apple cider
>
> about 3 cups sugar
>
> 3 teaspoons cinnamon
>
> 1 teaspoon ground cloves
>
> 1 teaspoon allspice
>
> ½ teaspoon nutmeg

Wash and quarter apples; cook slowly in cider until soft. Put through a food mill or sieve.

Add sugar and spices and return to stove. Cook over low
heat, stirring constantly until thick, about one hour.
Test to see that butter "sheets" off the spoon.

Pour into sterile jars. Seal at once.

Makes three pints.

Cranberry Chutney

Wonderfully Christmassy. This chutney goes well
with chicken or turkey, roast pork, or meatloaf.
It should be sweet and hot and sour, all at once,
and it keeps well, if there's any left after Christmas.

> 6 cups fresh cranberries
>
> 1 cup golden raisins
>
> 2 cups light brown sugar
>
> ½ cup white vinegar or lemon juice
>
> 1 cup chopped onion
>
> 1 cup chopped apple
>
> 2 cinnamon sticks
>
> 2 inches fresh ginger, finely chopped
>
> ⅛ teaspoon ground cloves
>
> 1 small fresh chili (optional)

Combine all ingredients in enamel or stainless-steel pot,
bring to a boil and then simmer slowly, stirring
often for about forty-five minutes. Chutney should
be slightly thickened. Be careful not to let it stick
or burn.

Spoon into sterilized jars and process ten minutes in
boiling water bath or refrigerate.

Makes about three pints.

Mary's Pineapple Rhubarb Jam

This is good enough to eat by the spoonful and
heavenly on toast or toasted muffins.

> 3 to 4 cups chopped fresh or
> frozen rhubarb
>
> 1 large (16-ounce) can crushed pineapple
>
> 5 cups sugar
>
> 1 bottle commercial pectin or box
> Sure Jell

In a large enamel kettle, bring fruits and sugar to a boil
and cook to mix flavors.

Add pectin or Sure Jell and boil to the jelling stage, or
follow Sure Jell directions.

Ladle into sterile jars.

Note: This jam may take several weeks to set.

Makes about seven jars.

Spicy Peach Jam

Here's the one to make when that basket of peaches
is waiting on the porch and the family is full of
cobbler.

> 8 cups peeled, chopped ripe peaches
>
> 6 cups sugar
>
> 1 teaspoon salt
>
> 2 inches fresh ginger root, grated
>
> 2 sticks cinnamon
>
> 1 teaspoon whole cloves
>
> 1 teaspoon whole allspice

Tie cloves and allspice in a cheesecloth bag.

Combine peaches and sugar. Let stand for a few hours, then cook carefully until thick, about one hour, stirring often to prevent scorching.

Remove spice bag and cinnamon sticks.

Pour, boiling hot, into sterile jars. Pour a thin layer of hot parafin on top.

Makes about eight jars.

Tomato Jam

This is better than ketchup on hamburgers, excellent with broiled chicken, and exotic with meatloaf.

3 cups molasses

2 cups brown sugar

2 cups vinegar

1 teaspoon ground cloves

1 teaspoon cinnamon

1 teaspoon allspice

1 teaspoon salt

5 pounds ripe tomatoes

3 cups raisins

Make syrup of molasses, sugar, vinegar, and spices. Cook one-half hour.

Peel and chop tomatoes and add to syrup; cook slowly for at least two hours, stirring often, and watching to see that it does not stick and burn.

Add raisins and cook one hour longer.

Pour, boiling hot, into sterile jars and seal.

Makes about six pints.

Spiced Cranberries

This simple, old-fashioned relish is a beautiful color and a good combination of sweet and spicy. It goes well with roasts, meat, or poultry.

2½ cups sugar

½ cup water

2 two-inch sticks cinnamon

1 teaspoon whole cloves

2 tablespoons lemon juice

grated rind of 1 lemon

4 cups fresh or frozen cranberries

Combine sugar, water, spices, lemon juice, and rind and boil together for five minutes.

Add cranberries and cook slowly until all skins pop open.

Seal in sterile jars.

Makes four cups relish.

PICKLES

Adeline Snell's Mustard Pickles

"We always had them with baked beans on Saturday night," says Adeline Snell of Gorham, Maine, about her mustard pickles. Mrs. Snell still uses the recipe her mother, Gladys Jordan Irving, and grandmother, Adeline Moses Jordan, used in Portland, Maine. This pickle is a very colorful concoction—red with peppers, green with tomatoes and cucumbers, and yellow with spices. Mrs. Snell makes it late in the fall, using the last "little cucumbers that no way are going to be ripe," and harvesting the cauliflower.

1 quart very small cucumbers
(if not small, cut into chunks)
1 quart green tomatoes (small
if possible), sliced
2 quarts button onions, peeled
2 large heads cauliflower, cut into
small pieces
4 green peppers, chopped
1 red pepper, chopped

Dressing:

1 cup flour
1 tablespoon dry mustard
2 tablespoons turmeric
cider vinegar to blend
2 to 2½ cups sugar

Make a brine of four quarts water and one cup salt. Pour over vegetables. Set overnight. Drain, cover with water, and bring to a boil.

Make a dressing for the pickle, as follows:

Mix flour, dry mustard, and turmeric and blend to a paste with the cider vinegar. Add to this the sugar and enough vinegar to make seven cups.

Cook until thick, stirring so as not to scorch.

Add drained vegetables and heat through.

Bottle, cap, and process five to ten minutes in hot water bath.

Makes ten to twelve pints.

Anna Bebo's Chili Sauce

Cooks in West Haven, Vermont, are still passing around Anna Bebo's recipe for chili sauce.

1 peck ripe tomatoes
6 ripe green peppers
3 sweet red peppers
9 onions
2 cups white sugar
4 cups vinegar
2 tablespoons salt
2 teaspoons cinnamon
2 teaspoons cloves
2 teaspoons allspice

Peel and chop tomatoes. Chop other vegetables.

Combine all other ingredients in a big kettle and cook slowly for forty-five minutes, stirring often.

Put in jars and seal. Process in hot water bath for thirty minutes.

Makes about six pints.

Green Tomato Pickles

This is a sweet chopped pickle, wonderful with hamburgers or meatloaf. The recipe is from western Vermont.

2 pecks green tomatoes

1 cup salt

3 pints chopped onions

1 pint chopped green peppers

6 cups light brown sugar

1 quart vinegar

1 teaspoon allspice

½ teaspoon ground cloves

3 teaspoons cinnamon

Slice tomatoes and let stand overnight with salt,
then drain.

Put tomatoes through food chopper with other vegetables.

Cook with sugar, vinegar, and spices in a large kettle
until thick.

Process in sterile jars fifteen minutes.

Makes about eight pints.

Slide Easy Pickles

This is a very old Vermont recipe for sweet
cucumber pickles, also called Tongue Pickles. The
cucumber is seeded and cut up so that it does look a
bit like tongues. And they do slide down the throat.

About 8 or 10 large cucumbers

3 cups brown sugar

1½ cups white or apple vinegar

1 tablespoon cassia buds

1 tablespoon whole cloves

1 tablespoon allspice berries

Peel and seed large cucumbers and cut into three-inch
lengths. Soak them in a weak brine overnight,
then drain.

Parboil cucumbers in equal parts vinegar and water until
they are transparent.

Add brown sugar, whole cloves, cassia buds, and allspice
and cook, stirring often, for about an hour or
until done.

Jar and process as usual.

Makes about four pints.

Thousand Island Pickles

This is a Vermont version of a well-known pickle
which keeps well and goes wonderfully with meat
in any form. Or baked beans. Like the Slide Easies,
it need not be made with special pickling cucumbers.

8 to 10 large cucumbers

3 cups sugar

3 cups vinegar

1 teaspoon celery seeds

1 teaspoon turmeric

1 tablespoon salt

Peel and seed the cucumbers and chop into one-inch
pieces.

Make a syrup of sugar, vinegar, and spices and cook the
cucumber pieces in it until they are transparent.

Place in jars and process ten minutes in a hot
water bath.

Makes about four pints.

Rosy Spiced Crabapples

Nothing is prettier on a holiday table than rosy, long-stemmed crabapples. They are extremely simple to put up.

4 pounds crabapples

4 cups sugar

3 cups vinegar

1 cup water

3 cinnamon sticks

1 tablespoon whole cloves

1 tablespoon whole allspice

Choose unblemished, well-formed crabapples. Do not peel or stem. Some cooks prick the apples with a long needle to prevent them from cracking.

Boil sugar, vinegar, water, and spices together in a large kettle. Turn off heat; add crabapples and let stand overnight.

Drain crabapples and pack into sterile pint jars.

Cook syrup until it is reduced to the consistency of honey.

Pour carefully over fruit in jars.

Seal and process in hot water bath ten minutes.

Makes six pints.

Watermelon Rind Pickles

My grandmother used to make these. Tasting them today brings back memories of summer evenings on the back porch in Hyannis, eating watermelon and then carrying the rind inside for her to save for making pickles.

Rind from one large watermelon, cut into one-inch chunks, about 3 quarts

1 tablespoon powdered alum

6 cups sugar

2 cups vinegar

3 cinnamon sticks

3 tablespoons whole cloves

1 tablespoon ground nutmeg

Prepare rind by paring off outside green skin, leaving a bit of the pink flesh, and cut into chunks. Cover and soak overnight in water with two tablespoons salt and the juice and rind of one lime. Drain, rinse, and cover again with water.

Heat to boiling point, then drain again.

Cook sugar and vinegar with spices to make a syrup. Add rind chunks and cook about two hours until syrup is thick and pickle tender.

Spoon into sterile jars, seal and cool.

Makes about six pints.

Special Treats

Molasses Popcorn Balls

Kids love popcorn balls, and few adults can resist their chewy sweetness. They can be hung on the Christmas tree or tied into a circular wreath. This recipe is from Verna Crane Whipple who was born

and still lives on Stowe Mountain Road in
New Hampshire's Hillsborough Upper Village.

"We always have molasses popcorn balls
at Christmas. I keep them in the house to give to
everyone who comes in. I used to wrap them in
colored cellophane paper—red and green and blue
and yellow. That was real pretty, but now I put each
one in a small plastic bag and tie red ribbons on.
My mother, Grace Lovejoy Crane, who grew
up in Lempster, used to do over a hundred every
Christmas for community parties."

> 1 cup molasses
>
> 1 cup sugar
>
> 1 teaspoon vinegar
>
> 2 tablespoons butter
>
> few grains soda
>
> ½ teaspoon vanilla
>
> 3 big poppers full of corn;
>
> about 6 quarts

Boil molasses, sugar, and vinegar until a little, when
  tried in cold water, rattles on the side of a glass.
  Then add butter, soda, and vanilla. Stir and cool
  slightly. Pour over corn.

Shape into balls a little larger than a tennis ball with
  buttered or floured hands.

Store the popcorn balls in a cool place.

Makes about twenty large popcorn balls.

Green Tomato Mincemeat

This is a very old recipe, tried and true. Processed in
glass jars, it keeps well on the cupboard shelf, ready
to be turned into a rich holiday pie. Raisins may be
added when making pies.

> 2 quarts chopped, green tomatoes
>
> 2 quarts chopped apples
>
> 1 pound raisins
>
> 1 pound currants
>
> ½ cup butter
>
> ½ cup vinegar
>
> 2 cups molasses
>
> 5 cups brown sugar
>
> 2 teaspoons salt
>
> 2 teaspoons cloves
>
> 4 teaspoons cinnamon
>
> 1 teaspoon nutmeg

Cover the tomatoes with water, then scald and drain.

Combine with apples, raisins, currants, suet, vinegar,
  molasses, and spices in a big enamel kettle.

Cook all together until thick and dark, stirring frequently.
  This should take about two hours or more.

Pour into sterile jars, seal, process in hot water bath
  ten minutes.

Makes about eight pints.

Old-Fashioned Mincemeat

Using a combination of lean beef and suet, this is a very flavorful mincemeat and a generous gift. A pie using this mincemeat is really a full meal, very sustaining. Venison may be used instead of beef.

2 pounds lean beef (or venison)

1 pound suet

about 6 cups chopped, tart apples

2 cups brown sugar

1 cup molasses

4 cups cider

1 cup vinegar

2 cups of the meat stock

1 tablespoon cinnamon

1 tablespoon salt

1 teaspoon allspice

1 teaspoon nutmeg

1 teaspoon cloves

2 pounds raisins

2 pounds currants

Cover meat and suet with water and cook until tender, about two hours.

Cool in cooking water, remove fat that congeals on top. Remove meat and reserve liquid and suet.

Chop meat and mix it with peeled, cored, chopped apples. There should be twice the quantity of apples.

Cook with sugar, molasses, cider, vinegar, and spices in a large enamel kettle for about two hours. Add currants and raisins and cook one hour more. Add suet and two cups stock.

Pour into sterile jars and process in hot water bath one and one-half hours.

Makes about five quarts.

Auntie Esther's Doughnuts

Auntie Esther was Esther Hill, a native of Pembroke, New Hampshire, who when I was a little girl, lived down the street. I always thought she was a marvelous cook. These days when Auntie Esther's buttermilk doughnuts show up at a party, they're usually the work of Robert Fowle. Try them tossed in cinnamon sugar in a paper bag as soon as they're drained.

2 eggs

1 cup sugar

1 cup buttermilk

½ teaspoon nutmeg

¼ teaspoon baking soda

¼ teaspoon salt

¼ teaspoon baking powder

scant 4 cups flour

Cream eggs and sugar; add buttermilk.

Sift dry ingredients together to make dough stiff enough to roll out about one-half inch thick. (Cool if necessary.)

Cut out doughnuts with doughnut cutter.

Fry in deep fat heated to 365°F until golden brown.

Drain on paper.

Makes about eighteen doughnuts.

Classic Chocolate Fudge

Perhaps the best Christmas present of all. Imagine holding a well-wrapped box of fudge in your hands, smelling it, noting the weight of it, then opening it and tasting the first piece. A Christmassy variation is to substitute pistachios for the walnuts and decorate with candied cherries, although for the classic chocolate lover, it would not be necessary. This recipe never fails.

> ¾ cup milk
>
> 2 ounces unsweetened chocolate
>
> 1½ cups sugar
>
> 2 tablespoons light corn syrup
>
> dash of salt
>
> 2 tablespoons butter
>
> 1 teaspoon vanilla
>
> 1 cup chopped walnuts

Butter an 8 x 4-inch pan with plenty of butter and set aside.

Melt chocolate and milk together in a large, heavy saucepan.

Add sugar, corn syrup, and salt and cook, stirring constantly, until it comes to a boil.

Stir no more. Cook without stirring until a candy thermometer reads 234°F or mixture forms a soft ball in cold water.

Remove pan from heat. Pour vanilla and place butter on top of the fudge mixture and let it cool undisturbed until thermometer reads 110°F or lukewarm.

Beat with wooden spoon or mixer on low speed until creamy, just when it begins to lose its shine and thicken. Fold in nuts, spread in pan, and let cool.

Makes about one pound.

Maple Walnut Fudge

If you know someone – particularly someone now far from the sugarbush – who has a taste for this fudge, nothing makes a better gift.

> 2 cups maple syrup
>
> 2 tablespoons light corn syrup
>
> ¾ cup light cream or half-and-half
>
> ½ teaspoon salt
>
> 1 teaspoon vanilla
>
> 1 cup chopped walnuts
>
> walnut halves for decoration

Stir maple syrup, corn syrup, cream, and salt together in a large, heavy saucepan and heat to a boil, stirring constantly. Then cook without stirring to the soft ball stage, when candy thermometer reads 238°F.

Remove from heat. Cool to lukewarm or 110°F without stirring.

Beat with wooden spoon or electric mixer on low speed until fudge loses its gloss and thickens. (Take turns with family members; this step takes time.)

When it is thick, stir in vanilla and nuts and spread quickly in an 8-inch square, well-buttered pan. Score into squares and set a walnut half on each. Cool. Cut into squares.

Makes about one pound of fudge.

Candied Apples

These, like the popcorn balls, are natural gifts for children and may make an appearance at a children's Christmas party. However, I have found that adults, too, relish the sweet-tart combination of a fresh candied apple.

> 10 well-formed apples
>
> 2 cups sugar
>
> ¾ cup light corn syrup
>
> 1⅓ cup evaporated milk
>
> ¼ teaspoon salt
>
> 1 teaspoon vanilla

Mix the sugar, corn syrup, milk, and salt in a heavy two-quart saucepan.

Boil until sugar dissolves, then cook slowly to 230°F on a candy thermometer or until a thick syrup spins a two-inch thread when spun off a spoon.

Remove from heat. Stir in vanilla. Cool briefly.

Insert wooden skewers in stem ends of apples and dip in caramel, working quickly, twisting to cover well, tipping pan as needed. Keep caramel hot so that it will cover thinly. If it gets cool, heat it again with a little more milk.

Cool apples on a well-buttered cookie sheet.

Makes ten candy apples.

Seasonal Libations and Holiday Drinks

Since colonial times, New Englanders have warmed their hearts and toasted the seasons with a variety of festive drinks. Many of these traditional libations are rum-based; others can be stirred and savored just as well without alcoholic spirits. Some of these drinks are served piping hot, just the thing to welcome a traveler in from the cold, and all of them answer the need for something specially festive to offer guests at Christmastime.

Lamb's Wool

This is a traditional Christmas punch, apple cider-based, that may have originally been made with crabapples. Its name comes from the apple pulp floating on the surface of the punchbowl.

4 to 6 apples

2 quarts apple cider or ale or a mixture

¼ cup light brown sugar

2 cinnamon sticks

¼ teaspoon nutmeg

¼ teaspoon ginger

Bake the apples in a 400°F oven until they are very soft.

Cool, peel, and mash apples.

Combine apple pulp with cider and/or ale, brown sugar, and spices. Heat thoroughly. Strain.

Serve hot.

Makes twelve or more servings.

Sparkling Christmas Punch

Vodka may be added to this punch.

2 quarts cranberry juice

juice of 2 oranges

juice of 2 lemons

2 quarts cider

2 quarts seltzer or soda water

Mix, chill, and serve.

Makes twenty servings.

Mulled Wine

This spicy wine punch was traditionally made with claret. Use any good-quality, full-bodied red wine.

2 cups water

12 cloves

1 teaspoon nutmeg

¼ cup sugar

juice of ½ lemon

2 bottles red wine

Boil spices in water with sugar and lemon juice. Strain. Add wine and heat slowly. Serve hot, garnished with clove-studded orange slices.

Makes about twelve servings.

Ruby Punch

This cold, fragrant punch is more complex and stronger than mulled wine.

2 bottles of red Burgundy or other red wine

1 cup ruby port

½ cup kirsch

juice of 6 oranges

½ cup sugar

2 quarts of seltzer or soda water

Mix all ingredients except seltzer. Pour over ice in a punch bowl. Add bubbly water.

Serves fifteen to twenty.

Eggnog

6 eggs

½ cup sugar

2 cups milk

1½ cups dark rum or other spirits,
    if desired

2 cups heavy cream

grated nutmeg

Combine eggs, sugar, and milk in the top of a double
    boiler and cook slowly over low heat until it forms a
    soft, smooth custard.

Chill. Stir in liquor and cream.

Pour into punch bowl and generously grate nutmeg
    on top.

Makes ten to twelve servings.

Fresh Cranberry Punch

A delicious, hot, nonalcoholic punch.

4 cups fresh or frozen cranberries

3 quarts water

10 whole cloves

4 cinnamon sticks

1 cup orange juice

½ cup lemon juice

2 cups sugar

Combine cranberries, water, and spices in large kettle.
    Simmer about fifteen minutes. Strain.

Add fruit juices and sugar. Stir until sugar dissolves.

Serve hot in mugs.

Serves twelve to fifteen.

Syllabub

This is a mild version of the old-fashioned creamy
punch. It can also be made with hard cider or brandy.

2 cups white wine

1 cup sugar

grated peel of one lemon

½ cup lemon juice

2 cups heavy cream

Dissolve sugar in wine, add lemon juice, and lemon peel.

Whip cream and fold into mixture. Chill.

Garnish with grated nutmeg.

Makes ten servings.

Wassail

Another traditional New England Christmas punch imported from Old England. The word comes from the Old Norse for "to be in good health." Traditionally, toasts to good health and good luck are made with cups of wassail, which can be based on wine or ale, and flavored with sugar and spices and usually apples.

> *6 small, tart apples*
>
> *1½ quarts ale*
>
> *1 cup light brown sugar*
>
> *3 whole cloves*
>
> *2 teaspoons mixed ginger, cinnamon,*
> *   and nutmeg*
>
> *peel of one lemon*
>
> *1 pint Malaga wine or sherry*

Bake apples in a 375°F oven until they are soft.

Combine one-half of the ale with sugar and spices and lemon peel and simmer for ten minutes.

Add the rest of the spirits and heat but do not boil. Pour over baked apples to serve.

Makes ten servings.

Fabulous Holiday Parties

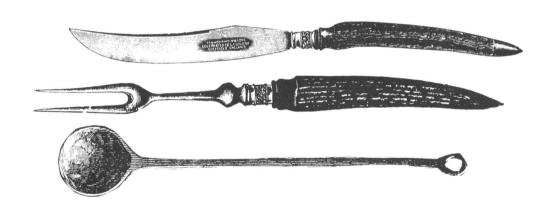

Now Christmas is come,
Let's beat up the drum,
And call all the neighbors together,
And when they appear,
Let us make them such cheer
As will keep out the wind and the weather.

Washington Irving

A certain madness possesses the minds of most of us at about Christmastime. No matter how busy we are with presents for children, mailing cards and packages, decorating the house and the tree, cooking special foods for planned holiday meals, we are possessed with the compulsion to become hosts. It's part of the spirit of the season. The urge to share food, to extend our hospitality, to get together with friends we see often and friends we never see often enough becomes stronger and stronger. It can only be eased by the giving of a party. The season presents many occasions for parties. You may find yourself planning more than one. Here, at any rate, are some suggestions for making merry.

Holiday Open House

Every Christmas I find myself planning a fairly big party for friends, neighbors, and colleagues. It's often held on a weeknight a week or two before Christmas, and so people can drop in after work or shopping I say, "Come between six and nine." It's very informal, but festive and fun, and to be successful, depends on things being ready well ahead of the first guest. This is a cocktail buffet with some dishes substantial enough to stand in for supper for those guests who want that. I buy a dozen loaves of bread at the best local bakery to go with the fish and meat dishes. Because of my own heritage, some of the dishes have a Scandinavian accent, and it's important to have plenty of sweets, even at a cocktail party. People really like them – it must be the time of year.

Cheese Stars

Boston Chicken Liver Spread

Salmon Mousse

Chopped Herring in Sour Cream Sauce

Sliced Baked Ham with Rye Bread and Mustards

Blueberry-Lemon Cake

Almond-Frosted Fruitcake

Tiny Chocolate Partycakes

Assorted Christmas Cookies

Cheese Stars

These can be made in any shape or twisted into straws, but stars are perfect for a Christmas party. Roll out on a floured pastry cloth, and store tightly covered when cooled. They can also be made ahead of time and frozen.

1½ pounds sharp cheddar cheese

½ cup butter

3 cups sifted flour

1 teaspoon paprika

½ teaspoon salt

½ teaspoon cayenne

Grate cheese and mix with butter.

Mix in flour, paprika, salt, and cayenne and cut as
for pastry.

Roll out to about one-quarter-inch thickness on pastry
cloth or lightly floured surface and cut with star-
shaped cookie cutters.

Bake on ungreased cookie sheets at 400°F for eight to
ten minutes or until golden brown.

Makes from four to six dozen stars, depending on size of
the cutters.

Boston Chicken Liver Spread

The cognac is optional in this recipe, the chopped fresh parsley is not. Serve with fresh rye bread. This recipe was given to me by a native of Boston's old West End, Dorothy Beretz Kutz.

1½ pounds chicken livers

½ cup butter

1 chopped onion

2 hard-boiled eggs

salt and ground black pepper to taste

½ cup fresh parsley, chopped fine

1 tablespoon cognac

Saute livers and onion in butter until onion is
translucent and livers are just cooked through.

Put liver and onion mixture through meat grinder
with eggs.

Add parsley, salt, pepper, and cognac (optional). Season
to taste.

Chill and garnish with parsley.

Serves twelve as an appetizer.

Salmon Mousse

This simple jellied mousse is a personal favorite. Every time I think "party," I reach for canned salmon and a fish-shaped copper mold. Some of my friends would be disappointed if I ever broke the habit.

1 large (15½-ounce) can red
  or pink salmon

1 envelope unflavored gelatin

½ cup boiling water

½ cup mayonnaise

3 tablespoons fresh lemon juice

½ teaspoon paprika

1 teaspoon bottled tabasco sauce

½ teaspoon salt

2 tablespoons chopped scallions

2 tablespoons chopped, fresh dill

Drain the canned salmon (reserving the juice) and pick
  out the skin and bones. Set aside.

Soften gelatin in one-quarter cup of the reserved juice.

Add boiling water and stir to dissolve. Cool slightly.

Add mayonnaise, stir well, and then add lemon juice,
  paprika, tabasco, and salt. Chill until mixture is
  slightly thickened, about the consistency of egg
  whites.

Using blender or food processor, combine salmon and
  mayonnaise mixture in small batches and process
  until smooth.

Fold in scallions and dill. Pour into oiled fish or other
  mold and chill until firm.

Turn out and decorate with dill; use black olive for
  fish's eye.

Serve with crackers or bread.

Serves ten to twenty as an hors d'oeuvre.

Chopped Herring in Sour Cream Sauce

This recipe has Scandinavian antecedents and a New England accent. We eat much less herring than our grandparents did and most of it at Christmas parties. A pretty salad to serve with thin-sliced rye bread.

2 cups chopped boiled potatoes

2 cups chopped boiled beets

½ cup chopped scallions or mild onion

2 finely chopped herring fillets

½ teaspoon salt, if herring is not salty

freshly ground pepper

¼ cup chopped fresh dill

1 cup sour cream

3 tablespoons beet juice

Combine all ingredients, taste for seasoning, and chill
  12 hours, stirring at least twice.

To serve, mix one cup sour cream with three tablespoons
  beet juice and fold into herring and vegetables.

Serves twelve as an appetizer.

Sliced Baked Ham with Rye Bread and Mustards

Buy or bake a good-sized ham and slice it carefully into thin slices. (Don't leave the slicing for your guests to do.) Arrange it on a platter, supply plenty of fresh rye bread and at least two varieties of mustard. By providing this dish you can rest assured that even the fussiest children will be fed and peace will reign at the party.

Blueberry-Lemon Cake

Blueberries from the freezer, of course. Baking and eating this cake will bring back memories of the breezy August day spent on a mountainside happily picking wild berries. It is a simple pound cake with a tangy lemon glaze.

> 1 cup blueberries
>
> 2 cups sifted all-purpose flour
>
> ½ cup butter or margarine
>
> 1 cup sugar
>
> 2 eggs
>
> ½ cup milk
>
> 1½ teaspoons baking powder
>
> ¼ teaspoon salt
>
> 1 tablespoon grated lemon peel

Flour blueberries and set aside.

Cream butter or margarine and sugar. Add eggs one at a time and beat until light and fluffy.

Add dry ingredients alternately with milk, mix gently.

Fold in floured blueberries and grated peel.

Bake sixty-five to seventy minutes in 8-inch tube pan which has been well buttered and lined with waxed paper. Test with toothpick to be sure it's cooked through—frozen berries slow the cooking time.

Cool about ten minutes in pan, then remove from pan and prick top with toothpick.

Brush with hot Lemon Glaze.

Serves twelve to sixteen.

Lemon Glaze

> ¼ cup sugar
>
> ¼ cup fresh lemon juice
>
> 1 tablespoon grated lemon peel

Combine in small saucepan and heat to dissolve sugar.

Cool cake completely before serving.

Almond-Frosted Fruitcake

Under the frosting on this distinguished family fruitcake is a thin layer of almond paste. It should be baked well ahead of time and set aside in a cool place to ripen. Frost it a day or two before the party and decorate with cherries, almonds, and citron.

¾ cup butter

¾ cup dark brown sugar

4 eggs

2 cups flour

pinch of salt

¼ teaspoon nutmeg

¼ teaspoon cinnamon

¼ teaspoon allspice

¼ teaspoon cloves

½ pound currants

½ pound sultanas

2 ounces chopped candied orange peel

¼ cup candied cherries, halved

¼ pound chopped almonds

3 tablespoons brandy

1 small, grated apple

For the icing:

1 pound almond paste

1 pound confectioners' sugar

2 egg whites

½ teaspoon glycerine

Beat last three ingredients together until of spreading consistency.

For the cake:

Cream butter and sugar together until light and fluffy.

Beat in eggs, one at a time.

Fold in flour, salt, and spices.

Add remaining ingredients in the order listed, beating well.

Pour into well-buttered, floured, 8-inch cake pan at least three inches deep.

Bake in 350°F oven one hour. Lower oven to 325°F and bake another hour and a quarter. If cake browns too fast, cover with brown paper or aluminum foil. Test center to be sure it is cooked through.

Cool before removing from cake pan.

When thoroughly cool, cover with almond paste rolled out to thin dough. Shape to cover cake completely.

Frost with plain icing and decorate before serving. Slice very thin.

Serves twelve to twenty.

Tiny Chocolate Partycakes

It's a good rule that every party buffet has to include at least one chocolate dessert. These light little cupcakes are good party fare. Each is one delicious mouthful.

¾ cup butter

1 cup sugar

5 egg yolks

4 squares unsweetened chocolate

1½ cups flour

1 teaspoon baking powder

¼ teaspoon salt

5 egg whites

Cream butter and sugar; beat in egg yolks.

Add melted, cooled chocolate and blend well.

Add dry ingredients a little at a time, and, finally, fold in egg whites beaten to soft peaks.

Spoon batter into small cupcake tins with paper liners.

Bake in 350°F oven about fifteen minutes or until done.

Frost with chocolate butter frosting.

Makes twenty-four tiny cupcakes.

CHILDREN'S CHRISTMAS PARTY

Christmas is, after all, especially for children and if there are any children in your life you are likely to get swept up into the excitement of Christmas with a special fervor. If you have the opportunity to give a party for children, you are in for a treat—especially if you're prepared. Whenever possible at a party that includes all age groups, give the littlest ones their own table and provide them with a variety of appetizers that can be served at room temperature, such as grapes, raisins, nuts, and bread sticks. If there's a cookie tray, party fare for small children might begin with such snacks and end with cookies and milk.

Packaging and presentation are as important for children as for adults. Old-fashioned gingerbread people, each with a child's name written on in white frosting, can mark places at the table. A holiday mix of nuts and raisins, cashews, and dried sugared cranberries in gold-foil muffin cups might go a long way toward delighting a crowd of children dressed up for Christmas, who might then be served small portions of a simple, festive meal like this one.

GINGERBREAD PEOPLE

RED AND GREEN PEPPER STICKS

PIGS IN BLANKETS

MOLDED GELATIN SALAD

SANTA CLAUS CUPCAKES

CRANBERRY-ORANGE PUNCH

Gingerbread People

No Christmas is quite complete without a batch or two of gingerbread, whether cut into the shapes of little people or of stars and trees, Santas and sleighs, hearts and bells. Here is a master recipe that makes dozens of cookies. Once mixed, the dough keeps very well in the refrigerator for months. Bake some now, bake some later.

> 1 pound brown sugar
>
> 1¼ pounds butter
>
> 2 pounds sorghum molasses
>
> 2 teaspoons baking soda
>
> 10 cups flour
>
> 1 teaspoon cinnamon
>
> ¼ teaspoon ground cloves
>
> ½ teaspoon cardamom
>
> ¼ teaspoon allspice
>
> grated rind of 1 orange
>
> grated rind of 1 lemon
>
> ½ pound almonds, blanched and
>
>   finely ground

Heat brown sugar, butter, and molasses until dissolved.

Cool, then add two teaspoons baking soda dissolved in a little hot water.

Add remaining ingredients.

Mix well. Chill, then roll thin.

Cut out gingerbread figures. Store remaining dough.

Bake cookies in 325°F oven for eight to ten minutes or until lightly browned. (They burn easily.)

Makes ten dozen or more, depending on size of the cookies cut.

Pigs in Blankets

The pigs are frankfurters, their blankets pieces of bread or biscuit wrapped around to give fingers something to hold. Although this classic dish is often – and quickly – made with prepared hot-roll mix, it can also be done very easily with a simple biscuit dough. Use miniature frankfurters or cut up regular ones into three pieces. If using prepared dough, roll it out, wrap it around the meat, let it rise, and bake at 450°F about fifteen minutes.

For the biscuit dough:

2 cups flour

2 teaspoons baking powder

1 teaspoon salt

2 tablespoons shortening or butter

¾ to 1 cup milk

Mix dry ingredients and sift twice.

Work in shortening or butter with pastry blender, knife, or fingers until it forms rough crumbs.

Add liquid bit by bit, mixing to make a soft dough.

(Amount will vary according to the characteristics of the flour.)

Knead on a floured board, then roll out to about one-half- to three-quarters-inch thickness.

Cut squares and wrap them around the frankfurters. Press to close.

Bake on buttered cookie sheet in 450°F oven for about fifteen minutes.

Makes about twelve biscuits or blankets.

Molded Gelatin Salad

This can be molded in small individual molds, either round or in shapes such as bells and trees, or in a single large mold. Children like it.

1 cup ground cranberries

1 cup sugar

1 package unflavored gelatin

1 cup hot water

1 cup diced unpeeled apple

1 cup crushed pineapple and its juice

½ cup chopped nuts

1 cup chopped celery

Combine cranberries and sugar.

Dissolve gelatin in hot water. Add fruits and stir.

When it begins to thicken, stir in celery and nuts.

Pour into mold and chill until firm.

Santa Claus Cupcakes

These are perfect plain cupcakes. Frosted in pink, decorated with a coconut beard, bright eyes, and a wide smile they will be easily recognized as homage to the patron saint of Christmas.

For the cupcakes:

I always use paper muffin cups to line the tins. Look for the decorated ones at Christmastime.

> ½ cup butter or shortening
>
> 1 cup sugar
>
> 2 cups cake flour
>
> ¾ teaspoon salt
>
> 2¼ teaspoons baking powder
>
> 2 eggs
>
> 1 teaspoon vanilla
>
> ¾ cup milk

Sift dry ingredients together.

Put all ingredients except half of the milk into a mixer bowl.

Beat slowly until just mixed, then beat two minutes at medium speed.

Add the rest of the milk.

Beat one minute.

Bake in muffin tins lined with paper cups in a 375°F oven for twenty-five to thirty minutes.

Makes eighteen cupcakes.

For the frosting:

> ⅓ cup cream cheese
>
> 1 cup confectioners' sugar
>
> 1 teaspoon vanilla
>
> 1 tablespoon milk, or more

Beat all ingredients together until of spreading consistency.

Tint frosting pale pink with cherry juice, strawberry syrup, cranberry syrup, or a drop of red food coloring.

Frost cupcakes and decorate with candies and coconut.

Cranberry-Orange Punch

> 1 quart cranberry juice
>
> 1 quart orange juice
>
> 1 quart seltzer or club soda

Mix and chill.

Makes three quarts, serves about ten.

Tree-Trimming Supper for the Neighbors

This is a simple, informal meal for that night when neighbors arrive, by car or on foot, to drop off packages and advise the children on decorating the tree. A big tray of cheeses and sliced carrots, celery, radishes, and whatever vegetables look good in the market is set up in the living room near the tree and the boxes of ornaments just carried down from the attic. The cabbage soup is hearty and filling, and it smells so good that it lures everyone into the dining room for a sit-down meal, even if it is eaten in shifts as the doorbell rings and new visitors arrive. Rye bread sticks are popular with all generations and the pear-cranberry crisp is a delightful seasonal dessert.

Cheese Tray with Fresh Raw Vegetables

Winter Cabbage Soup

Rye Bread Sticks

Pear-Cranberry Crisp with Whipped Cream

Winter Cabbage Soup

Ham hocks give this soup a rich, traditional flavor, but in a vegetarian household, they may be omitted and ginger may be added to the tomato-garlic stock to give additional flavor. This is a homey soup and stands up well to substitutions. Make plenty to have some left over for lunch.

> 1 cup white beans, soaked overnight, or
>   good-quality canned white beans
> 2 to 3 ham hocks
> 1 large head cabbage, shredded
> 3 large onions
> 1 pound carrots
> 3 stalks celery
> 2 sweet red peppers
> 2 to 3 cloves garlic
> 1 twenty-eight-ounce can whole
> tomatoes and liquid
> 6 cups water
> sliced lemon
> chopped parsley

If using dried beans, soak them overnight, then drain. Good-quality canned beans may be used successfully.

Chop vegetables and add to soup kettle with ham hocks, beans, tomatoes, water, and salt and pepper to taste.

Cook slowly until beans are soft and ham hocks have given their flavor to the vegetables — at least two hours.

Serves about twelve.

Rye Bread Sticks

These flavorful soft bread sticks are easy to make and easy to eat.

> 1 tablespoon or package fresh dry yeast
>
> ¼ cup butter
>
> 3 tablespoons honey
>
> ½ teaspoon salt
>
> 2 cups whole rye flour
>
> 1 cup white bread flour
>
> 1 cup whole wheat flour
>
> 1 tablespoon plus caraway seeds
>
> 1 egg yolk beaten with 1 tablespoon water

Dissolve yeast in one and one-quarter cups lukewarm water.

Add butter, honey, salt, rye flour, and one tablespoon caraway seed and beat until smooth.

Cover and let rise about forty-five minutes.

Work in rest of flour, one-half cup at a time, then turn out onto floured board and knead until smooth and elastic.

Divide dough in half and shape into long rolls. Cut each roll into about twelve pieces; twist into rope or crescent shape.

Let rise, covered, on greased baking sheets for about thirty minutes.

Brush with beaten egg yolk and sprinkle with more caraway seeds.

Bake about fifteen minutes in 400°F oven.

Cool under cloth. Store in airtight container.

Makes about twelve sticks.

Pear-Cranberry Crisp

This dessert is equally delicious made with apples. Serve with whipped cream or vanilla ice cream.

> 6 to 7 large ripe pears, preferably
>
>   Comice or Bartlett
>
> 1½ cups cranberries, roughly chopped
>
> 1 cup sugar
>
> 1 teaspoon cinnamon
>
> ½ cup flour
>
> pinch of salt
>
> ½ cup butter
>
> 1 cup rolled oats
>
> ½ cup chopped walnuts or pecans

Pare, core, and slice pears. Toss gently with cranberries, half the sugar, and cinnamon. Spread the fruit in a buttered baking dish.

Combine remaining sugar and cinnamon with flour, salt; cut in butter as for pastry, then stir in oats and nuts. Spread this over fruit.

Bake in 375°F oven about forty-five minutes or until pears are tender and crust is lightly browned.

Serves eight to ten.

Carolers' Reward

After an exhilarating round of caroling, friends don't want to separate. Instead, plan a simple dinner that can be waiting at home, put on some background music, and celebrate by the fireside.

Toasts with Herbs and Cheese
Veal Stew with Mushrooms
Steamed Rice
Mixed Red and Green Salad
Individual Quince Tarts

Toasts with Herbs and Cheese

This simple hors d'oeuvre can be assembled and ready to slip under the broiler when the first guests arrive. By the time the first glasses of wine are poured, these crisp savories can be passed with them.

> 1 loaf French bread, sliced thin
>
> ½ cup soft butter
>
> ¼ cup grated cheese
>
> 1 teaspoon minced garlic
>
> 1 tablespoon chopped parsley
>
> 1 tablespoon minced fresh basil
>
>   or tarragon

Mix butter, cheese, and herbs and spread on slices of bread.

Broil until brown and crisp.

Serves eight to ten.

Veal Stew with Mushrooms

This festive, hearty stew actually improves in flavor by being made ahead of time and reheated when the carolers come in the door.

> 1 inch peeled ginger root
>
> 3 cloves of garlic
>
> 1 tablespoon dried hot pepper flakes
>
> 4 scallions, white tips only
>
>   (save green tops)
>
> 3 pounds boneless veal for stew, cut into
>
>   2-inch cubes
>
> ⅓ cup flour
>
> salt and pepper
>
> 3 tablespoons vegetable oil
>
> 1 cup chicken stock
>
> 1 cup dry white wine
>
> 1 pound fresh mushrooms
>
> ½ cup heavy cream
>
> 2 tablespoons lemon juice
>
> 2 cups parboiled small white onions

Chop ginger, garlic, pepper, and scallions in food processor or finely by hand. Set aside.

Dredge veal in flour seasoned with salt and pepper. In a Dutch oven or heavy flameproof casserole, brown meat in oil, adding more oil if necessary. Remove browned meat from casserole as it is done and set aside.

Lower heat and saute ginger and garlic mixture in remaining oil and flour, stirring well and scraping the pan. Pour in stock and wine, correct seasoning, and bring to a simmer.

Add browned veal and cook over low heat forty-five minutes.

Stir in sliced mushrooms and simmer ten minutes longer. Remove meat and reduce sauce for about ten minutes, then add cream and lemon juice. Add parboiled onions. Return meat to the sauce and stir to coat.

Garnish with minced green scallion tops, additional minced ginger root, and very finely sliced red peppers.

Serve hot with rice.

Serves six to eight.

Mixed Red and Green Salad

You'll need 10 to 15 cups mixed fresh salad greens, both red and green to include chicory, romaine, raddicio, or red cabbage.

4 tablespoons olive oil

2 tablespoons fresh-squeezed lemon juice

salt to taste

Toss lettuces together and season with oil, lemon juice, and salt.

Serves eight to ten.

Individual Quince Tarts

Ever since I discovered how to cook quinces, I have been enamored of them. Nothing smells more delicious when cooking or takes on such a beautiful rosy color. Neither apples nor pears, quinces can be used whenever either of those fruits is called for, or combined with them. They are very tart until cooked in sugar syrup; for these holiday tarts, they are almost candied.

For the filling:

8 large quinces

2 cups sugar

3 cups water

2 cinnamon sticks

Peel and core quinces. Cook them carefully in a mixture of sugar and water, spiced with the cinnamon sticks, for about two hours, or until they are soft. Reserve. (Quinces in syrup can be kept in the refrigerator for months.)

For the pastry:

1 cup flour

⅛ teaspoon salt

8 tablespoons butter

1 to 2 tablespoons ice-cold water

Mix flour and salt in a bowl; cut in butter.

Sprinkle water on top of roughly mixed dough and work it with a fork or your fingers until it makes a ball, adding more water if necessary.

Roll out and line eight 3½-inch tart pans.

Partially bake tart shells, pricked and weighted with

beans in 350°F oven for about ten minutes.

To assemble:

Drain quinces and boil syrup to reduce it.

Carefully slice quinces and arrange them in the tart shells,

hiding any broken pieces under the perfect slices.

Paint quince slices with reduced syrup, which will be

jelly-like, and bake in 400°F oven ten to twenty

minutes or until pastry is brown and filling is

shining and set.

Serves eight.

DESSERT PARTY

Everyone loves desserts, and special Christmas desserts are in a class by themselves. For once, skip the cheese and carrot sticks and plan a party starring sugarplums and sweet concoctions exclusively. Does the idea seem irresistible? Plan it for an afternoon or evening just before or after Christmas, set up a buffet table to show off the splendid assortment, include a selection of teas and coffees, and perhaps some chilled champagne or sauterne. It's a good idea to provide large dessert plates and cut everything into small portions. Remember, most people love chocolate. I include three chocolate desserts to balance the nonchocolate ones.

GINGERED PEAR CHEESE TART

RICH, EASY PUMPKIN PIE

DEEP-DISH CRANBERRY-APPLE PIE

FAVORITE CHOCOLATE LAYER CAKE

STRAWBERRY TRIFLE

MAPLE MOUSSE

CHOCOLATE MACAROON PUFFS

CHOCOLATE WALNUT BARS

Gingered Pear Cheese Tart

Elegant and delicious. This is a dessert that takes a bit of planning in that you have to have the pear preserves on hand, but it is very fast to assemble once you do.

Buttery Tart Pastry

> 1 cup flour
> ½ cup butter
> 1 teaspoon ground ginger
> 2 tablespoons sugar
> ½ teaspoon salt
> few tablespoons ice water

Cut butter into flour mixed with ginger, sugar, and salt.

Mix with ice water, using as little as possible.

Chill for one-half hour or more.

Roll out on floured pastry cloth and fit into a 9-inch tart pan.

Partially bake at 350°F for ten to fifteen minutes to use for the tart.

Gingered Preserved Pears

If not used for the gingered pear tart, these preserves are delicious served on dessert pancakes with a dollop of sour cream or whipped sweet cream. And, of course, they're also good on ice cream.

> 1 dozen ripe pears, the best of the season
> 2 cups sugar
> 1 cup brown sugar
> 2 inches of fresh ginger root, shredded
> 1 lemon, seeded and sliced thin

Peel and slice the pears.

Cook in sugar and water to cover, spice with ginger and sliced lemon. Cook until syrup is thick and pears are tender.

Seal in sterile quart jars. Refrigerate.

Makes two quarts.

To make the tart filling:

> 2 eggs
> 8 ounces cream cheese
> ½ cup sugar
> ½ cup cream
> pinch of salt
> ½ cup toasted almond pieces

Beat eggs, add cream cheese, and beat until smooth.

Add sugar, salt, and cream. Beat well.

Pour into partially baked tart shell.

Bake in 350°F oven for about forty minutes and then turn off oven. Let cool.

Drain pear preserves and set pears aside.

Boil syrup until thick.

Arrange pear slices over cheese mixture in tart shell and spoon on glaze.

Sprinkle with toasted slivered almonds.

Chill.

Serves six to eight.

Rich, Easy Pumpkin Pie

This can be made in minutes in a blender or bowl. Real Yankees—such as my husband—like to pour additional maple syrup over this sweet pie.

> 2 cups pumpkin puree
>
> 1 cup maple syrup
>
> 4 eggs
>
> 1 cup heavy or light cream
>
> ½ teaspoon ginger
>
> ½ teaspoon cinnamon
>
> ½ teaspoon salt
>
> 1 9-inch unbaked pie shell

Combine all ingredients, blend well, and pour into pie shell.

Bake in preheated 425°F oven for ten minutes. Reduce temperature to 325°F and bake an additional thirty-five minutes.

Cool. Chill or serve at room temperature.

Serves eight.

Deep-Dish Cranberry-Apple Pie

Traditional deep-dish fruit pies use lots of fruit and have no bottom crust. Leftovers keep well, although don't count on leftovers with this tart-sweet pie made with fresh apples and canned cranberries. This simple dessert is enhanced by vanilla ice cream.

> 1 recipe buttery tart pastry (page 63)
>
> 1 sixteen-ounce can whole
>
>   cranberry sauce
>
> ¼ cup raisins
>
> 8 to 10 crisp, medium apples
>
> ½ cup sugar
>
> ½ teaspoon cinnamon
>
> 3 tablespoons butter
>
> 2 tablespoons milk
>
> sugar

Mix cranberry sauce and raisins and set aside.

Peel and slice apples and mix with one-half cup sugar and cinnamon.

Layer in a deep baking dish, alternately with cranberry mixture. Top with bits of butter.

Cover with buttery tart pastry. Brush with milk and sprinkle with sugar.

Bake in 400°F oven for about forty-five minutes or until pastry is golden brown.

Serves eight.

Favorite Chocolate Layer Cake

This is my interpretation of the famous "Wellesley Fudge Cake." I had a taste for chocolate cake long before I matriculated at Wellesley. I have made this recipe so often that I can get it in the oven in less than twenty minutes. This cake is fine-grained, especially delicious when very fresh, keeps well, and is unusually dark because of the brown sugar and coffee.

❄ Christmas Rum Balls • Sissy Shattuck's Filled Cookies ❄
• Saucepan Fruit Bars with Lemon Glaze • CHRISTMAS COOKIES

Cranberry Cheesecake ▪ CHRISTMAS CAKES

❋ Pineapple Pecan Loaf ▪ FESTIVE HOLIDAY LOAVES ❋

❄ Classic Chocolate Fudge ■ SPECIAL TREATS ❄

❄ Rich, Easy Pumpkin Pie ■ DESSERT PARTY ❄

❄ Favorite Chocolate Layer Cake with Dark Chocolate Frosting ▪ DESSERT PARTY ❄

❄ Oyster Stew • Christmas Cornbread • Indian Pudding • OLD-FASHIONED CHRISTMAS EVE SUPPER ❄

❄ Winter Fruit Cup ▪ CHRISTMAS BRUNCH AT HOME ❄

❄ Roast Turkey with Old-Fashioned Bread Stuffing ❄
• Fresh Cranberry-Orange Relish • CHRISTMAS DINNER FOR THREE GENERATIONS

3 ounces unsweetened baking chocolate

⅓ cup strong coffee

¾ cup butter (or margarine)

2¼ cups packed brown sugar

2 eggs

1 teaspoon vanilla

2 cups sifted flour

1 teaspoon baking soda

½ teaspoon salt

1 cup strong coffee

Melt chocolate in one-third cup coffee over very low heat, stirring. When melted, set aside to cool slightly.

Meanwhile, measure dry ingredients and sift them together.

Cream butter and brown sugar very well.

Add eggs one at a time and beat well.

Add vanilla and then blend in chocolate. Beat well.

Add dry ingredients alternately with one cup coffee, mixing just enough to combine, by hand or on lowest mixer speed.

Pour into well-buttered, 9-inch cake pans lined with buttered wax paper.

Bake in 350°F oven thirty-five to forty minutes or until test shows that it is cooked through. Do not remove cake too soon or it will fall.

Cool ten minutes in pan, then remove and cool on racks. Frost with Dark Chocolate Frosting.

Makes one 9-inch cake; serves ten.

Dark Chocolate Frosting

4 tablespoons butter

3 ounces unsweetened chocolate

3 cups sifted confectioners' sugar

¼ teaspoon salt

½ cup strong coffee

1 teaspoon vanilla

Melt chocolate in a double boiler.

Soften butter. Stir in melted chocolate.

Add sifted confectioners' sugar and salt alternately with coffee and beat to desired consistency. Beat in vanilla.

Frosts top and sides of 9-inch cake.

Strawberry Trifle

Trifle, also known as Tipsy Parson, is a very old New England dessert. It lends itself to enormous variation and is easily enlarged to feed a crowd. This recipe is good for Christmastime because it is one of the best uses of frozen strawberries and good for a party as it has to be made ahead of time. If you don't like the taste of sherry, it can be omitted.

1 plain sponge cake or purchased pound cake

2 pints frozen strawberries, thawed

¼ cup sherry

3 cups custard

½ pint heavy cream, whipped

½ cup toasted almonds

To make the sponge cake:

>1 cup sugar
>
>2 eggs
>
>1 teaspoon vanilla
>
>1 cup cake flour
>
>1½ teaspoons baking powder
>
>½ teaspoon salt
>
>½ cup hot milk
>
>2 tablespoons butter

Beat eggs very well. Add sugar and beat very well again. This should be very pale and quite thick.

Sift dry ingredients together twice.

Add alternately with butter melted in the milk, beating until smooth. Batter will be thin.

Pour into well-buttered, 8-inch square pan.

Bake at 350°F for about thirty minutes or until golden brown and done when tested. Cool.

For the custard:

>2 cups light cream
>
>4 egg yolks
>
>⅓ cup sugar
>
>¼ teaspoon salt
>
>1 teaspoon vanilla

Mix egg yolks, sugar, and salt in top of double boiler.

Add scalded cream, stirring constantly, and cook until mixture coats a spoon, about fifteen minutes.

Add vanilla. Cool.

To assemble trifle:

In a pretty, deep dish, place slices of cake to form a layer.

Spoon strawberries with their juice on top and sprinkle with sherry.

Spoon on a layer of custard and repeat until dish is filled and all custard and cake have been apportioned.

Spread whipped cream on top and sprinkle with almonds.

Garnish with two or three reserved strawberries, if possible.

Maple Mousse

Incredibly rich and creamy, this easy frozen mousse can be made well ahead of time. To serve at a party, set it in a bowl of ice and provide very small portions. John K. Farrar of Carter Hill Road, Hillsborough, who provided this recipe, is a maple syrup maker himself.

>5 eggs
>
>1¼ cups maple syrup
>
>⅛ teaspoon salt
>
>2 cups heavy cream
>
>walnuts to garnish

Beat eggs lightly in top of double boiler.

Heat syrup and gradually add to eggs, beating vigorously.

Add salt and cook until thick, stirring constantly.

Cool.

Fold in whipped cream. Garnish with chopped walnuts and a ring of walnut halves.

Freeze.

Serves eight.

Chocolate Macaroon Puffs

These airy, meringue-like cookies are both tempting and satisfying, both chewy and crisp.

>2 egg whites
>
>½ cup sugar
>
>¼ teaspoon salt
>
>½ teaspoon vanilla
>
>6 ounces chocolate chips, melted
>
>1½ cups grated coconut

Beat egg whites until foamy.

Melt chocolate over hot water. Cool.

Slowly sift in sugar, beating after each addition until smooth.

Continue beating until mixture stands in peaks.

Add salt and vanilla; fold in melted chocolate.

Fold in coconut.

Drop by teaspoonsful onto cookie sheets covered with thick paper.

Bake in 300°F oven about twenty minutes.

Cool slightly before removing cookies from paper.

Makes two dozen.

Chocolate Walnut Bars

These are sweet and delicious. Cut into bars about one inch wide and two inches long, each will disappear in two bites.

For the first layer:

>1 cup butter
>
>2½ cups flour
>
>½ teaspoon salt
>
>½ cup sugar

For the filling:

>3 eggs
>
>½ cup flour
>
>1½ cups corn syrup
>
>1 teaspoon vanilla
>
>¼ teaspoon salt
>
>⅓ cup melted butter
>
>2 cups chocolate chips
>
>2 cups chopped walnuts

Prepare 10 x 15-inch baking pan by buttering well.

Combine ingredients for first layer as for pastry and spread in pan. Press down evenly.

Bake in 375°F oven fifteen minutes.

Beat eggs well; add corn syrup, vanilla, salt, and melted butter. Then stir in chocolate and nuts.

Pour onto baked cooled crust and bake in 350°F oven thirty to forty minutes or until firm around the edges.

Cool, then cut into bars.

Makes about three and a half dozen bars.

Victorian-Style Christmas Tea

Relaxed, comfortable "at-homes" have been popular in New England since the nineteenth century, especially at holiday times. Linda Ashford, Executive Director of the Kimball-Jenkins Estate in Concord, New Hampshire, tells us that invitations to such events might have gone out by mail or word-of-mouth, and she has supplied a typical menu. Of the recipes supplied, the punch recipe would have been the most treasured and most jealously shared—each family took special pride in their own punch. The Kimball-Jenkins house is a perfect example of the Victorian gothic style, was lived in by three generations of a prominent New Hampshire family, and is now open to the public both for tours and special events serving Victorian-style foods.

Buttered Rum Pound Cake

Marble Cake

Christmas Cookies

Russian Tea Cakes

Raisin Scones with Whipped Butter

Hot Rum Punch or Earl Grey Tea

Buttered Rum Pound Cake

1 cup softened butter

2½ cups sugar

6 eggs, separated

3 cups flour

½ teaspoon baking soda

8 ounces sour cream

1 teaspoon vanilla

1 teaspoon lemon extract

½ cup sugar

Cream butter, then beat in two and a half cups sugar until light and fluffy. Separate eggs; add yolks one at a time, beating well after each addition.

Sift together flour and baking soda.

Add to creamed mixture alternately with sour cream, beginning and ending with dry ingredients.

Stir in vanilla and lemon extract.

Beat egg whites until foamy; gradually add one-half cup sugar, one tablespoon at a time, beating until it forms stiff peaks.

Gently combine egg whites with batter.

Pour into a greased and floured 10-inch tube pan.

Bake in 325°F oven for one and a quarter hours.

Cool for fifteen minutes in pan, then remove and cool on plate. While still warm, prick surface with a fork and glaze with Buttered Rum Glaze.

Makes one cake.

Buttered Rum Glaze

10 tablespoons butter

3 tablespoons dark rum

¾ cup sugar

3 tablespoons water

½ cup chopped walnuts

Combine first four ingredients in a saucepan and boil, stirring constantly, for about five minutes. Remove from heat and stir in walnuts.

Marble Cake

Use only the best quality chocolate for this cake, a great Victorian favorite which does, in fact, resemble marble or marbled Italian paper.

12 tablespoons butter

¾ cup sugar

3 eggs

1¼ cups flour

1 teaspoon baking powder

½ teaspoon salt

2 ounces semisweet chocolate

Cream butter and sugar until pale and thick, then gradually beat in eggs, beating well again.

Sift dry ingredients together and fold into creamed mixture.

Melt chocolate and trickle it in three rings over the cake batter, then feather it with a knife blade so that it is streaked but not muddy.

Butter and flour one 7- or 8-inch cake pan at least three inches deep.

Bake about one hour in a 350°F oven.

Cool on a wire rack.

Serves six to eight.

Christmas Cookies

This is a very old recipe for rolled cookies. Use Christmas cookie cutters in shapes of trees, stars, crescents, and wreaths. Cookies may be decorated or frosted, or left plain.

1 cup butter

1 cup sugar

2 eggs

½ teaspoon salt

½ teaspoon nutmeg

½ teaspoon cinnamon

nearly 3 cups flour

¼ cup milk

Cream butter and sugar together. Add eggs.

Add spices, then milk, and enough flour to make a stiff dough.

Chill, then roll out into a thin sheet and cut into shapes with a cookie cutter.

Bake at 375°F about ten minutes.

Makes about three dozen cookies.

MERRY CHRISTMAS

Russian Tea Cakes

1 cup butter

½ cup confectioners' sugar

1 teaspoon vanilla

2¼ cups sifted flour

½ teaspoon salt

¾ cup finely chopped nuts (walnuts or
almonds or a mixture)

additional confectioners' sugar

Cream butter, sifted confectioners' sugar, and vanilla.

Sift dry ingredients together and combine with creamed
mixture. Mix in nuts.

Chill for an hour or two.

Roll into one-inch balls and bake in 400°F oven for ten
to twelve minutes.

While still warm, roll balls in confectioners' sugar.

Makes about two dozen cookies.

Raisin Scones

Scones, warm, tender, and crusty, are as wonderful
on the tea table today as they were one hundred
years ago.

2 cups flour

2 teaspoons baking powder

½ teaspoon baking soda

2 tablespoons sugar

½ teaspoon nutmeg

½ teaspoon salt

½ cup butter

1 egg

¾ cup buttermilk or plain yogurt

1 cup raisins

1 egg white

cinnamon sugar

Mix dry ingredients together and cut in butter as for
pastry with knives or a pastry blender.

Combine slightly beaten egg and buttermilk or yogurt
with raisins; pour into dry mixture and mix only
until moistened.

On floured pastry cloth or board, knead about twelve
times. Pat into circle one-half inch thick.

Transfer to baking sheet. Brush top of cake with beaten
egg white and sprinkle with cinnamon sugar. Mark
off wedge-shaped pieces, cutting down about
halfway.

Bake in 400°F oven about fifteen minutes or until tops
are golden brown.

Makes twelve scones.

Hot Rum Punch

This is similar to the one served at the Kimball-Jenkins house, but not exactly the same. Feel free to vary it a little to give it your signature.

> 4 cups cranberry juice
>
> 2 cups pineapple juice
>
> 2 cups water
>
> 3 cinnamon sticks
>
> 5 cloves
>
> ¾ cup brown sugar

Combine in a coffee pot and perk.

Add dark rum to taste.

Serves about eight.

FAMILY CHRISTMAS FEASTS

More than for any other holiday, New England families gather at Christmas, and nearly every family keeps certain traditions. The Yankee community has long been ethnically diverse and, unlike the very first settlers, who did not celebrate Christmas, nineteenth- and twentieth-century immigrants have added their personal and national accents to the flavor of what we call an old-fashioned Christmas. Christmas Eve supper at home, usually a meatless meal, is the most important celebration for some families; for others, it is the morning meal or the daytime meal on Christmas Day. Among New Englanders today, there are many different "traditional" Christmas meals. Here are some of them, with special notice paid to the Italian, Polish, Greek, Finnish, and French-Canadian national traditions.

An Old-Fashioned Christmas Eve Supper

Few parts of New England are far from the sea, and Yankees have always relished seafood. There's a wonderful Marblehead tradition of serving boiled lobsters — and plenty of them — for dinner on Christmas day. The big pots are set to boil, a long trestle table is set up, covered with a dark green cloth, and the feast begins. A Nantucket woman says Christmas dinner should be Scalloped Oysters, baked with cream and crushed soda crackers. In my own family, the oysters were always served the night before Christmas, a tradition I keep today. A simple supper, just for the family might start with a rich oyster stew and end with that most old-fashioned of desserts, Indian Pudding.

Oyster Stew

Christmas Cornbread

Indian Pudding

Oyster Stew

Eating creamy oyster stew on Christmas eve is a tradition in many New England families, including my own. Letting the stew cool for an hour or so, then reheating gently, improves the flavor. Either you love oysters or you don't.

> 1 quart fresh oysters, shelled
>
> 1 cup cold water
>
> 1 quart light cream, half-and-half or a
> combination of milk and cream
>
> ¼ cup butter
>
> ½ teaspoon salt
>
> ¼ teaspoon white pepper

Pick over oysters carefully, separating bits of shell. Add water, cook gently until oysters plump up and begin to curl on edges.

Strain oysters and add to heated milk or cream.

Add strained oyster liquid, butter, salt, and pepper. Now let it rest for a while to let the flavor of the oysters come out in the cream.

Serve with oyster crackers or crusty French bread.

Serves four to six.

Christmas Cornbread

This is a hearty cornbread decorated for Christmas with red and green peppers.

> ¾ cup butter
>
> ¼ cup sugar
>
> 4 eggs
>
> 2 cups cream-style corn
>
> 1 cup shredded, sharp, Vermont cheddar
> or Monterey Jack cheese
>
> ½ cup chopped, mixed, red and green
> peppers (part hot, if you like)
>
> 1 cup cornmeal
>
> 1 cup flour
>
> 4 teaspoons baking powder
>
> ½ teaspoon salt

Cream butter and sugar. Add eggs one at a time, beating well after each addition.

Add the rest of the ingredients in the order listed.

Bake in a well-buttered 9 x 13-inch pan in a 300°F oven for about one hour or until golden brown.

Serves six to eight.

Indian Pudding

This pudding should be very soft. It is good served with pouring cream or vanilla ice cream.

> 5 cups scalded milk
>
> ⅓ cup corn (Indian) meal
>
> ½ cup molasses
>
> 1 teaspoon salt
>
> 1 teaspoon ginger

Pour milk slowly over meal and cook in a double boiler for twenty minutes.

Add molasses, salt, and ginger.

Bake in a well-buttered pudding dish in a 200°F oven for about two hours.

Serves eight.

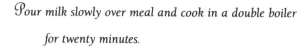

A French-Canadian Christmas Eve Supper

The French-Canadian tradition is a strong one in New England. A special Christmas Eve supper, served to the family after a day of fasting and their return from midnight mass, traditionally features pork pies, or tourtieres, served with winter vegetables such as carrots, onions, turnips, or cabbage, piccalilli relish, and according to Betty Lessard of the Manchester, New Hampshire Historical Society, "a very mild wine." Mrs. Lessard says the recipe for tourtiere doesn't vary a lot throughout New England; her own mother seasoned it with summer savory. Two recipes for tourtiere follow, one old-fashioned and one a bit modified by Grace St. Pierre Maynard of Albion, Rhode Island.

Philomene St. Pierre's Pork Pie

This is a traditional recipe.

2 pounds blade meat (or any pork)

1 pound veal or beef (veal has a

better flavor)

small clove of garlic, chopped fine

1 onion, chopped

salt and pepper to taste

Grind meat together, or ask your butcher to do it.

Put all ingredients together in a large kettle and cover
with about one cup water.

Simmer over low heat until water is evaporated and
meat is tender and moist, about two hours, stirring
occasionally.

Bake in regular pie crust, about fifteen minutes in 400°F
oven.

Makes enough filling for two average pies.

Grace Maynard's Pork Pies

Both Grace Maynard and her sister Anita have
tinkered with their mother's recipe until they are
satisfied with the results. Mrs. Maynard recommends
baking the pies a day in advance and then
reheating them. This enhances the flavor. She serves
tourtiere with salted or dill pickles and ketchup.

4 pounds ground pork

2 pounds lean ground beef

2 large onions, chopped

3 stalks celery, chopped

small clove of garlic, chopped extra fine

Add approximately an inch and a half of water to a large
kettle. Then add above ingredients and two

envelopes chicken or beef granules. Bring to a
boil, cover kettle, and simmer slowly till meat is
partially cooked, about one hour.

Uncover and simmer thirty minutes more. Add one
teaspoon salt (or to taste), scant teaspoon pepper,
three-quarter teaspoon sage. Simmer another thirty
minutes, uncovered.

Remove from stove. If very fat, spoon off some of the fat.
(Let cool a bit; it's easier to skim off fat when it has
congealed.)

Add about one cup fine bread crumbs. Blend thoroughly.

Place in regular pie shell, add top crust, and bake
approximately twenty minutes at 400°F, till crust is
done. (Meat filling can also be cooled, placed in
shell, and frozen unbaked.)

Makes enough filling for three 10-inch pies.

New England Italian-American Christmas Eve Supper

Traditionally, Italian-Americans eat no meat and
seven different dishes at their Christmas Eve feast.
Mary-Ann De Vita Palmieri and her husband
Anthony Palmieri of New Salem, Massachusetts, gave
me this menu after reminiscing about holiday
traditions from both of their families, as well as the
ones they have developed for their own three
children, Gioia, Cristina, and David. Both Palmieris

were born and raised in Boston and they agree that although the other dishes may vary from year to year, the Pasta Con Alici is absolutely essential.

CLAMS ON THE HALF SHELL

PASTA CON ALICI
(PASTA WITH ANCHOVIES)

STUFFED SQUID
(CALAMARI IMBOTTITI)

BACCALA CON CECI
(BAKED CODFISH
WITH CHICKPEAS)

BAKED EEL
(CAPATONE AL FORNO)

BROCCOLI WITH CHEESE SAUCE

ITALIAN BISCOTTI AND PIZZELLE
STRUFOLI

Mary-Ann Palmieri's Pasta Con Alici (Pasta with Anchovies)

Use fine pasta for this dish, either spaghettini or fresh angel hair pasta. It's a very simple dish, absolutely delicious, meant to be eaten quickly to silence a demanding appetite.

1 pound pasta

2 large cloves garlic

½ cup olive oil

1 can anchovies

chopped parsley

salt and pepper to taste

While pasta is cooking al dente, combine chopped garlic, oil, canned anchovies with their oil, parsley, and a bit of pepper. The anchovies are very salty, so you may need no additional salt.

Pour the sauce over the hot pasta and mix well.

Serves four to six.

Stuffed Squid (Calamari Imbottiti)

In the De Vita family, the stuffed calamari is cooked on top of the stove in a simple tomato sauce; in the Palmieri family, it is baked with oil only. This is Mary De Vita's recipe.

2 pounds squid

½ cup bread crumbs

1 stalk celery, chopped fine

1 clove of garlic, chopped

2 tablespoons grated Parmesan cheese

1 tablespoon or so olive oil to moisten

tomato sauce made of onions, celery, and tomatoes, seasoned with salt, pepper, basil, and garlic

Clean squid, removing eyes, outside skin, and intestines. Wash well under running cold water, drain.

Combine stuffing ingredients, moisten with olive oil, and

fill the cavity in each squid with stuffing. Fasten
   closed with toothpicks.

Cook on top of stove in tomato sauce until tender.

Serves six to eight.

Baccala Con Ceci (Baked Codfish with Chickpeas)

Dried, salted codfish is a traditional winter food in
most European countries and is prepared all over
Italy for Christmas. This version is from the Abruzzi
region, through Boston's North End. As Tony
Palmieri recollects this Christmas dish, it should be
quite liquid, "almost like a soup."

> 1 whole dried codfish, about 2 pounds
>
> ½ pound chickpeas, water to cover
>
> ½ cup olive oil
>
> 2 to 3 cups canned tomatoes
>
> 1 stalk chopped celery
>
> 1 chopped onion
>
> 1 tablespoon chopped parsley
>
> 1 clove garlic, minced

Soak codfish in cold water for two days, changing water
   four times. Drain and cut into serving pieces.

Soak chickpeas overnight and then cook slowly until
   tender.

Coat bottom of baking dish with two tablespoons of the
   olive oil; place fish and chickpeas in dish.

Make a simple marinara sauce with the rest of the oil
   and the tomatoes, celery, onion, parsley, and garlic.
   Pour over the fish and chickpeas and bake in

350°F oven until fish is tender and flavors are
blended, about one hour.

Serves six to eight.

Baked Eel (Capatone Al Forno)

This is a very traditional dish. Tony Palmieri
remembers his father bought the eel live in a North
End market, then kept it in the bathtub until it was
time to prepare this dish. One year, the eel's head
fell on the floor and the cat got involved. You may
choose to buy the eel already skinned and
decapitated.

> 1 skinned, washed eel
>
> ½ cup olive oil
>
> 1 clove garlic, chopped
>
> 2 tablespoons chopped parsley
>
> 1 cup bread crumbs
>
> salt and pepper
>
> 2 tablespoons white wine

Coil eel in oiled baking dish.

Mix garlic and parsley with bread crumbs and season
   with salt and pepper. Sprinkle eel with crumbs,
   moisten lightly with oil, and bake in a moderate
   oven, about 375°F until tender, about forty-five
   minutes.

Serves four to six.

Mary-Ann's *Biscotti*

This is the basic recipe for all Italian-style cookies. The dough can be shaped into twists, rings, or S-shapes or formed into balls or ovals. It can be flavored with anise and cut and toasted to make anise toasts. It can be rolled in sesame seeds or pignoli nuts. For Christmas, it is commonly frosted with a simple confectioners' sugar frosting and sprinkled with confetti-colored candy shot.

> 3 eggs
>
> ¾ cup sugar
>
> ½ cup vegetable oil
>
> 1 teaspoon vanilla or lemon extract
>
> 3 cups flour
>
> 3 rounded teaspoons baking powder

Mix eggs and sugar, then add oil, flavoring, and dry ingredients. (Dough will be stiff.)

Work into one-inch shapes.

Bake on greased cookie sheet in 400°F oven for about ten minutes or until lightly browned.

Frost with plain sugar frosting and sprinkle with colored confetti sugar.

Makes about four dozen cookies.

Pizzelle ("Snowflake Cookies")

These crisp, fragile cookies are baked in their own iron. Mary-Ann Palmieri uses an electric one that cooks two at a time in about thirty seconds.

> 6 eggs
>
> 1½ cups sugar
>
> 1 cup margarine, melted and cooled
>
> 2 tablespoons pure anise extract
>
> 3½ cups flour
>
> 4 teaspoons baking powder

Beat eggs, add sugar, and beat well.

Add melted, cooled margarine and anise flavoring.

Mix in flour and baking powder sifted together.

Bake in pizzelle iron.

Cool on racks.

Makes about six dozen cookies.

Mary-Ann Palmieri's Chocolate *Pizzelle*

A slightly untraditional version, but wonderful. Mix plain and chocolate pizzelle on a plate.

> 6 eggs
>
> 2 cups sugar
>
> 1 cup margarine, melted and cooled
>
> 3½ cups flour
>
> ½ cup unsweetened cocoa
>
> 4½ teaspoons baking powder

Beat eggs, add sugar, then melted and cooled margarine.

Sift flour, cocoa, and baking powder together and mix in.

Bake in pizzelle iron until crisp.

Cool on racks.

Makes about six dozen cookies.

Strufoli (Honey Clusters)

These can be made in individual portions or heaped up into a glistening, honey-coated pyramid. Either way, it's usually sprinkled with confetti sugar or pignoli nuts and powdered sugar.

> 2 cups flour
>
> 3 eggs
>
> ¼ teaspoon salt
>
> 2 cups oil
>
> 1¼ cups honey
>
> ½ cup sugar
>
> sugar for decorating

Sift flour onto pastry board or counter and make a well in the center. Break eggs into the well, add salt, and mix well with your hands, then knead until smooth.

Roll out dough on lightly floured board or pastry cloth to a thickness of about one-quarter inch. Cut into strips and then into small pieces, each about the size of a marble. Roll these pieces into balls.

Heat oil to 350°F and fry balls three at a time until golden brown, turning them with a wooden spoon. Drain and set aside.

Combine honey and sugar and cook about two minutes, stirring constantly, and watching closely so it does not burn.

Cook bits of fried dough in honey syrup, about one cup at a time, for about one minute. Remove with slotted spoon and cool enough to handle, then make small piles of five to seven each or one large pyramid.

Decorate with pignoli and powdered sugar or confetti sugar.

Serves about eight.

MASSACHUSETTS FINNISH-AMERICAN CHRISTMAS EVE SUPPER

The night before Christmas is sauna night in the traditional New England Finnish family. Visitors are offered a sauna and family members are invited to partake of the therapeutic hot bath as soon as they arrive from far and wide. (Some uncle or cousin would have started the wood fire burning much earlier, and the sauna would be ready by nightfall.) Supper after the sauna is a simple affair and, as always, coffee is available, as well as coffee bread (pulla), a simple pound cake, and butter cookies. On Christmas Eve, Finnish-Americans traditionally eat a dish of baked cod in a cream sauce (Lipeäkala); there would be some special cookies and Christmas tarts, and there would always be rice pudding.

Mummu's Lipeäkala

This is how my own mummu, or grandmother, Hilma Maki Wartiainen, of Westminster, Massachusetts, served the traditional salt cod on

Christmas Eve. Mummu was a wonderful cook, a professional cook after she retired from farming, who had a knack of making the simplest things taste of their essences.

> 2 pounds lutefisk or salted cod, soaked
> at least a week, or the same fish
> purchased presoaked from a
> fish market

Poach the fish in water, lift out onto a serving platter, and serve with white sauce with hard-boiled eggs.

Serves six to eight.

White Sauce with Hard-Boiled Eggs

> 4 tablespoons butter
> 4 tablespoons flour
> 1 teaspoon salt
> ½ teaspoon pepper
> 2 cups milk or light cream
> 6 eggs

To make a roux, melt the butter and add the flour, stirring constantly to avoid lumps. Add salt and pepper, then add milk or cream slowly, stirring constantly.

Hard-boil eggs, shell, and slice. Add to sauce.

Mummu's Riisipuuro

This traditional dish can be dressed up with whipped cream, baked with an almond (for good luck), or sweetened before serving. This, however, is the wholesome, traditional way Hilma Maki Wartiainen served it to her farming family on Christmas Eve in Massachusetts. Sometimes, at Christmas, a sauce of imported lingonberries or native raspberries is served with the pudding, but it is delicious with just butter and sugar.

> 1 cup uncooked white rice
> 6 cups milk
> ½ teaspoon salt

Cook rice in water to cover until it has absorbed all the water.

In a double boiler, cook the rice and milk over boiling water for at least two hours, stirring occasionally, adding more milk if necessary, until it is thickened and creamy.

Serve with butter and sugar to taste.

Serves six to eight.

Ann Anderson's Christmas Tarts

Finland-born Ann Anderson of Winchendon, Massachusetts, is said by some to be the very best Finnish cook in the whole Fitchburg area. At any rate, she is one of the very best. As Ann makes this tart pastry, it is almost as light as traditional puff pastry. Fillings of dates, apricots, or raisins instead of prunes are also good.

> ½ pound butter
>
> 1½ cups flour
>
> ⅝ cup ice water
>
> 1 pound dried prunes
>
> water to cover prunes
>
> ½ cup sugar or honey
>
> 2 tablespoons fresh lemon juice
>
> egg yolk, beaten with water
>
> sugar

Cut cold butter into flour with knives or pastry blender.

Add water, bit by bit, using as little as possible.

Roll out pastry to a rectangle about 12 x 9 inches. Fold into thirds, then roll into a square, fold, and refrigerate for an hour or two.

Roll out again, again fold into thirds, and roll into 12 x 9-inch rectangle. Fold and refrigerate overnight. ("You can do it a couple of times again while the kids are in bed," suggested Mrs. Anderson.)

Roll out the pastry and cut into 3-inch squares.

While pastry is resting, prepare prunes by cooking them in water until soft, draining them, and then mashing them with sugar and lemon juice.

Place a heaping tablespoon of prune filling in the center of each pastry square. Split the pastry from the four corners to within a half inch of the center and fold the dough up to form a pinwheel.

Brush the tarts with egg yolk beaten with water and sprinkle with a little sugar. Let them rest in the refrigerator about an hour.

Bake tarts in a 450°F oven for about ten minutes or until brown. Watch them closely because they brown fast. Cool on a rack.

Makes about two dozen tarts.

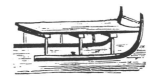

Ann Anderson's Christmas Bread

This is a traditional moist, rich coffee bread, my personal favorite among any on earth. Some Finnish-Americans eat this yeast coffee bread all year round, but everyone eats it at Christmastime, when it is sometimes formed into a cross, a star, or a pig shape and decorated according to the whim of the baker with cherries and nuts. Ann Anderson of Winchendon, Massachusetts, is widely known to make superb coffee bread. It is essential to use real butter and to spice the bread with ground cardamom seeds. To me, the smell of it is the smell of Christmas.

> 2 cups milk
>
> ½ cup sugar
>
> 1 teaspoon salt
>
> 3 eggs
>
> 1 teaspoon ground cardamom
>
> 2 packages dry or 2 tablespoons
>
>   fresh yeast
>
> ½ cup warm water
>
> 6 to 8 cups flour
>
> ½ pound butter

For the filling:

butter, sugar, cinnamon, raisins, nuts,
and candied or dried fruit to taste

For the frosting:

milk and confectioners' sugar, candied
cherries, and almonds

Heat milk to about 105°F, cool to lukewarm, add sugar.

Combine with salt, eggs, ground cardamom seed, yeast
dissolved in warm water, melted butter, and flour.
(The exact amount of flour will vary with the kind
used; Mrs. Anderson always uses King Arthur flour.)
Knead well by hand.

Shape into two small loaves or one very large one.
(Finnish coffee bread is often braided; for Christmas
you may want to shape a wreath. To shape, roll to
about one-half inch, then brush with melted butter
(up to an additional one-half cup) and sprinkle
with sugar, cinnamon, raisins, nuts, and fruits. Then
roll up and tuck ends under. With sharp scissors, cut
about halfway through the loaf all around, and let
it rise until double in bulk.

For a more traditional braid, roll three portions and
braid, tuck ends under, and brush with sugar and
cinnamon.

Let bread rise until doubled in bulk. Since this bread
rises only once, let it rise well.

Bake until light brown, about thirty-five minutes at
350°F. Do not overbake or it will dry out.

When slightly cool, frost with a thin icing of
confectioners' sugar and milk and decorate with
cherries and almonds.

Makes three braids or two wreaths.

GREEK-AMERICAN CHRISTMAS SPECIALTIES

Three generations of Greek-American New Englanders shared these special holiday recipes with us. The Greek-American community in and around Bridgeport, Connecticut, is a close-knit one. Three, four, even five generations are likely to gather at a holiday table there, and there are certain dishes that always appear. In addition, I include Angeliki Collias's recipe for stuffed grape leaves made in a pressure cooker, which she gave me nearly twenty years ago and which has never failed to please. Angeliki Collias lived for many years on Tremont Street, in the heart of Boston's South End Greek-American neighborhood, and was celebrated for her traditional cooking.

ROSE'S VASILOPITA (CHRISTMAS BREAD)

DIANE'S SPANAKOPITA WITH THREE FILLINGS

ANGELIKI COLLIAS'S DOLMADES AVGOLEMONO (STUFFED GRAPE LEAVES)

SOPHIE'S WALNUT BAKLAVA

Rose's *Vasilopita* (Christmas Bread)

This is a large recipe, but Rose Vatsivanos Vaggelopoulos of Bridgeport, Connecticut, often doubles it at Christmastime, to have plenty of this special bread to give away to family members. This bread is firm and it freezes well. The special spice, mahaleb or mahlepi, has a subtle but distinct flavor and is sold at most Greek specialty stores. If you can't find it, you might substitute anise. Mrs. Vaggelopoulos uses brick yeast which she buys at a Greek bakery.

> ½ pound fresh yeast
>
> 3 cups sugar
>
> 5 pounds flour
>
> ½ pound butter
>
> 1 rounded tablespoon solid shortening
>
> 2 cups milk
>
> 6 eggs at room temperature
>
> 1 teaspoon mahlepi
>
> 1 teaspoon salt
>
> beaten egg and sesame seeds to decorate

Dissolve yeast in eight ounces warm water.

Add one-quarter cup sugar and one cup flour. Mix to make a sponge, cover and set in a warm place — such as atop a stove with the oven set to about 250°F. Let rise until double.

Melt butter and shortening. Add milk. Add sugar.

Beat eggs and set aside.

Measure flour into large mixing bowl. Add mahlepi and salt.

Add other ingredients and mix by hand.

Knead dough one-half hour very slowly, then cover, and place in warm place.

Let rise until doubled in size. (This varies from one-half hour to one and a quarter hours.)

Punch down and divide into eight pieces. (Some cooks weigh the dough to make an even distribution.)

Roll out each piece into a long strip about one inch thick, then double the strip, and twist it to make a braid.

Let each loaf rise in a warm place until doubled in size. Note: unless your oven is large enough for all the loaves at once, put some to rise quickly on the stove and others to rise slowly (covered with plastic wrap) in a cooler place. This will allow a flow into the oven.

Brush each loaf with beaten egg and sprinkle with sesame seeds.

Bake in 350°F oven about thirty-five minutes or until firm and golden brown.

Makes eight loaves.

Diane's Spanakopita with Three Fillings

Diane Metsopoulos Connelly of Fairfield, Connecticut, is Rose Vaggelopoulos's granddaughter. Both she and her brother Peter are excellent cooks and interpreters of their mother's and grandmother's recipes. This recipe can be made in a large rectangular pan or used to make hors d'oeuvre-sized pitas. Buy fillo dough in the frozen-food section of supermarkets or in Greek specialty stores.

Cheese Filling:

> 6 eggs
>
> ¼ pound butter
>
> 1½ pounds cottage cheese
>
> ½ pound feta cheese

Beat eggs.

Melt butter.

Combine eggs and butter with cheeses in mixing bowl.

Spinach Filling:

> 2 ten-ounce packages frozen spinach
>
> 3 tablespoons butter
>
> 1½ pounds cottage cheese
>
> ½ pound feta cheese
>
> 6 eggs

Cook spinach in very little water until all the water evaporates.

Melt butter.

Mix butter and cheeses. Add beaten eggs.

Mushroom Filling:

> 4 large onions
>
> 4 tablespoons butter
>
> 3 pounds fresh mushrooms
>
> 1 tablespoon tomato paste
>
> 4 eggs
>
> salt and pepper to taste

Chop onions finely, then saute in butter until soft.

Add mushrooms and tomato paste. Cover and simmer over low heat for about an hour until mushrooms are dark.

Cool. Add beaten eggs and season to taste with salt and pepper.

To assemble one large pita:

> 1 pound of fillo dough
>
> ½ pound butter, melted

Butter a large rectangular pan, about 10½ x 14 inches.

Unroll fillo and place one sheet in pan. Brush with melted butter. (Note: the trick with fillo dough is to work fast. The dough is so fine that it dries out quickly and will crumble if dry.)

Place another piece on top of buttered fillo and brush with butter. Continue until you have used about half the fillo.

Spread filling and resume layering buttered fillo until it is used up.

Bake in 350°F oven for twenty to thirty minutes or until golden brown.

To assemble hors d'oeuvres-sized pitas:

> 1 pound fillo dough
>
> ½ pound butter, melted

Cut fillo dough in half widthwise.

Take one sheet, brush it with butter and fold it in half.

Place about one tablespoon filling at the top of the doubled sheet, center-fold each side over. Brush with butter.

Fold over again until you have a small rectangular package.

Brush top with butter. Place in buttered baking pan.

Bake twenty minutes in 350°F oven.

Makes about four dozen bite-sized pitas.

Angeliki Collias's Dolmades Avgolemono (Stuffed Grape Leaves)

These pressure-cooked stuffed grape leaves are tender and flavorful. The egg-and-lemon sauce balances the meat-and-rice stuffing.

> 1 jar or basket grape leaves
>
> 1½ pounds ground lamb
>
> 1 large onion
>
> 1½ cups rice
>
> 1 teaspoon salt
>
> ½ teaspoon pepper
>
> 1 teaspoon fresh or dried mint (thiasmos)
>
> 8 ounces chicken broth
>
> 8 ounces beef broth
>
> 3 eggs
>
> juice of 2 lemons

Rinse grape leaves if packed in brine.

Mix ground lamb, finely chopped onion, rice, and spices with one egg in a mixing bowl.

Assemble stuffed grape leaves by rolling about one tablespoon in each. Place point of leaf toward you, heap stuffing in the center, and fold the point over the stuffing. Then take each side and fold over the stuffing. Then roll and tuck under ends.

Pack the stuffed leaves seam down in a pressure cooker or a pan with a tight cover. Pour broths carefully over the tightly packed leaves.

Cook for ten minutes at ten pounds pressure or about one hour on top of stove.

Beat two remaining eggs. Add juice from two lemons and beat well; pour egg-and-lemon sauce over slightly cooled grape leaves.

Serve with more lemon.

Makes about three dozen stuffed grape leaves.

Sophie's Walnut Baklava

Sophie Metsopoulos of Fairfield, Connecticut, is the link between her mother Rose and daughter Diane. She makes this family recipe for the traditional, rich, honey-sweet dessert for special occasions, including Christmas.

> 2 pounds chopped walnuts
>
> 1 cup sugar
>
> 4 teaspoons cinnamon
>
> 2 pounds fillo dough
>
> 1¼ pounds sweet butter
>
> whole cloves for decoration

Melt butter.

Mix nuts and sugar with cinnamon and set aside.

Open fillo and divide into quarters.

Butter a 12 x 17-inch pan and spread fillo in it, brushing each leaf with melted butter. You must work fast so it doesn't dry out.

When one-quarter of the dough is layered in pan, spread layer of nuts and sugar mixed with cinnamon, then resume layering fillo, brushing each leaf with melted butter. Repeat.

End with layers of fillo. Brush top with butter.

With a sharp knife, cut small diamond shapes and place
a whole clove in the center of each.

Bake in 350°F oven about forty-five minutes or until
pastries are light brown on top, and move when you
shake the pan.

Note: Either pour hot syrup on cold baklava or cold
syrup on hot baklava. In other words, whichever
you make first determines the order of combination.

Serves twelve to fifteen.

Baklava Syrup

4 cups sugar

3 cups water

½ cup honey

juice of ½ lemon

Boil sugar, water, and honey together about fifteen
minutes or until a drop holds together on an
unvarnished fingernail.

Add lemon juice.

POLISH-AMERICAN CHRISTMAS EVE SUPPER

Traditionally, Yankee Polish-American families
gather for a special celebration on Christmas Eve.
The holiday meal, consisting of an odd number of
dishes, is served after someone sees the first star, on
a table set for an even number, with one setting left
empty for any stranger who might stop by.
Consultation with Maryann Zglobicki Sudol, of
Hillsborough, New Hampshire, and her husband's
mother, Mary A. Barsolowski Sudol of Hubbardston,
Massachusetts, produced this traditional menu.

PICKLED HERRING IN SOUR CREAM

CLEAR SEASONED MUSHROOM SOUP OR CABBAGE SOUP

PIEROGI

BAKED FISH WITH HORSERADISH SAUCE

SPICED RED CABBAGE

MARYANN'S RICE CAKE

Pickled Herring

Charles Sudol, Maryann's husband, starts well before Christmas to prepare herring and gives away many jars to herring fanciers among his friends. This is his recipe.

12 medium-sized, whole, salted herring

ice water

3 large Bermuda onions

2 tablespoons whole allspice

2 tablespoons sugar

enough vinegar to cover, diluted with

part water

1 bay leaf per jar

Soak whole salted herring in ice water for five to six hours.

Drain and filet.

Soak fillets for an additional two hours.

Slice onions and mix vinegar, sugar, and spices.

Cut herring into serving pieces and pack into jars, distributing onion slices and spices evenly. Pour on pickling liquid, add bay leaf, and let stand in refrigerator until use.

Serve on lettuce leaves with sour cream.

Serves twelve.

Clear Mushroom Soup

For a traditional Polish-American flavor, use dried black mushrooms such as the ones imported from Poland and found in many New England specialty shops.

For the broth:

3 pounds chicken backs, necks, and

wing tips

2 onions

3 ribs celery

2 carrots

½ cup parsley

Remove all visible fat from the chicken pieces. Quarter unpeeled onions and roughly chop other vegetables.

Place all ingredients in a large soup kettle and simmer for at least two hours. Strain off broth and season with salt and pepper.

For the soup:

2 ounces dried black mushrooms

2 quarts chicken broth

Soak the dried mushrooms in water to cover until they are soft.

Drain and chop mushrooms, reserving liquid.

Strain liquid well, add to broth.

Heat mushrooms in broth until flavors are well mixed and soup is piping hot.

Season to taste.

Serves ten to twelve.

Pierogi

Pierogi or pirogen, dough pockets stuffed with cheese, potato, or vegetable filling, are a beloved and traditional Polish dish. Maryann Sudol's recipe is for the basic dough and two fillings. The pierogi are delicious fried with additional onions and served with sour cream.

For the dough:

> 1 egg
>
> 1 cup flour
>
> ½ cup water
>
> pinch of salt

Mix flour, egg, and water and knead dough until it forms an elastic ball.

Roll out to about one-eighth-inch thickness and cut into 3-inch squares.

For potato stuffing:

> 4 to 6 potatoes
>
> 1 onion
>
> 2 tablespoons butter
>
> ¼ cup farmers' cheese
>
> salt and pepper to taste

Peel potatoes, cook, and mash.

Saute onion in butter until soft.

Mix potatoes and onions together with cheese and season to taste.

For sauerkraut stuffing:

> ¾ pound sauerkraut
>
> 2 to 3 tablespoons oil or bacon fat
>
> 1 onion, minced
>
> 2 tablespoons dried black
>
> mushrooms, softened
>
> salt and pepper to taste

Saute onion in oil or bacon fat until transparent.

Add mushrooms, sauerkraut, and fry until some of the sauerkraut becomes golden brown.

Season to taste with salt and pepper.

To assemble the *pierogi*:

Take one square of dough and place one teaspoon of filling in center. Fold and pinch to seal.

Cook in boiling water with a little oil until they rise to the surface.

Drain and cool on waxed paper. (At this point the pierogi can be refrigerated or frozen.)

When ready to serve, fry pierogi with onions until golden brown and serve with melted butter or sour cream.

Baked Fish with Horseradish Sauce

New England Polish-Americans use local fish such as haddock or cod for this dish. Choose any firm, white-fleshed fish.

> 3 to 4 pounds fish
>
> 4 tablespoons butter
>
> salt and pepper to taste

Arrange the fish in a buttered baking dish.

Bake in 300°F oven for about one hour, basting

frequently with the butter.

Serve with horseradish sauce.

Serves eight to ten.

Horseradish Sauce

    1 cup fresh or bottled grated horseradish

    2 medium beets

    2 tablespoons sugar

    2 tablespoons vinegar

Cook beets, drain, and puree.

Mix with other ingredients, season to taste, and chill.

Spiced Red Cabbage

A very satisfying and tasty dish. I also like the tang
a few tablespoons of aged balsamic vinegar adds.
This dish is wonderful with roast chicken or turkey.

    1 head red cabbage

    4 tablespoons butter

    1 large onion, chopped

    1 apple, chopped

    ¼ cup raisins

    ¼ teaspoon cloves

    2 tablespoons lemon juice

    1 tablespoon sugar

    ¼ cup chopped walnuts

Shred cabbage and steam it until nearly cooked.

Saute with onions in butter. Add remaining ingredients,

    except nuts, in order, and cook until flavors have

    mixed.

Stir in chopped nuts just before serving.

Serves about eight.

Maryann's Rice Cake

This rich, old-fashioned cake is a Christmas favorite
of the Sudol family. It's sweet and wholesome.

    2 cups rice

    5 cups water

    pinch of salt

    ½ pound sweet butter

    8 ounces cream cheese

    2 eggs

    1 cup sugar

    1 cup sultanas

    1 teaspoon vanilla

    1 cup milk

    1 cup flour

    ¼ teaspoon baking powder

Boil rice, salt, and water together until rice is cooked and

    water is gone.

Add butter and cream cheese and mix well.

Make batter of remaining ingredients, then combine

    with rice mixture.

Pour into a buttered 9 x 13-inch pan.

Bake in 375°F oven until golden brown, about one to

    one and a half hours.

Serves twelve.

Christmas Brunch at Home

Christmas morning often begins quite early—especially in a household with children—and is a time of lingering over cups of coffee, opening presents, making phone calls, and sharing family gossip. It's a good idea to plan something substantial for breakfast, which may be available buffet-style or may be eaten in shifts.

Winter Fruit Cup
Blueberry Muffins or Cranberry Muffins
Christmas Raisin Buns
Scrambled Eggs Three Ways

Winter Fruit Cup

"Take what you have . . ." is an old New England rule of cooking and it applies to concocting a fruit cup, especially in the winter. It's not really necessary to have a recipe, only an idea of what you like. When you visit your market, look carefully for whatever fruits are plentiful and look ripe and sweet. You may find good strawberries or ripe pineapple to add to the basic fruit cup. You may find a melon, and kiwi fruit, now commonly available, adds a touch of green. At any rate, most citrus fruits are in season and crisp native apples are still available. This recipe is only a guide.

2 apples, cored and diced

2 oranges, seeded, peeled, and sliced

1 grapefruit, seeded, peeled, and sliced

½ pound seedless grapes

1 large or 2 small bananas, sliced

1 pint basket strawberries

2 kiwi fruit, sliced

¼ cup honey

2 tablespoons fresh-squeezed lemon juice

2 tablespoons fresh-squeezed orange juice

Prepare fruit with an eye to appearance and combine in a large glass bowl.

Mix honey, lemon juice, and orange juice. Pour over fruit.

Let stand in refrigerator a few hours, or overnight.

Serve with sour cream, if desired.

Serves six to eight.

Blueberry Muffins

Frozen blueberries make this family favorite easy to produce on Christmas morning. Even small children are likely to eat three muffins—at least the children I cook for do. Paper muffin cups make it faster by eliminating buttering the tins.

1½ cups flour

½ cup sugar

3 teaspoons baking powder

½ teaspoon salt

1 egg

½ cup milk

½ cup melted butter

1 cup blueberries

Sift dry ingredients together.

Mix well-beaten egg with milk. Add all at once to dry
ingredients and stir just enough to moisten.

Just before completely blended, add melted butter, and
fold in blueberries.

Spoon into paper-lined muffin cups.

Bake in 400°F oven twenty to twenty-five minutes.

Makes twelve muffins.

Cranberry Muffins

Add raisins and/or chopped nuts if you like. These
are pretty and not too sweet.

    1 cup fresh or frozen cranberries,
        roughly chopped
    ¾ cup sugar
    1¾ cups flour
    2 teaspoons baking powder
    ½ teaspoon salt
    1 egg
    ¾ cup milk
    3 tablespoons melted butter

Chop or grind cranberries; mix with half the sugar.

Sift sugar with remaining dry ingredients.

Add combined egg, milk, and melted butter.

Stir only to mix.

Fold in cranberries, nuts, and raisins, if you like.

Bake in lined or buttered muffin tins in 425°F oven for
about twenty-five minutes.

Makes twelve muffins.

Christmas Raisin Buns

These sweet raisin buns are perfect for Christmas
morning because you mix them the night before.
Overnight, they rise in the refrigerator (or a cool
room). In the morning, you can shape the rolls, give
them a quick rise, and serve them to the family, with
or without a simple frosting of confectioners' sugar
and milk. The smell of them baking should stir
appetites.

    1 cup milk, warmed
    2 packages dry yeast
    ⅓ cup sugar
    1 teaspoon salt
    ½ cup melted butter
    1 egg
    about 3 cups flour
    1 teaspoon cinnamon
    1 cup raisins

For the frosting:

    confectioners' sugar
    milk

The night before:

Stir warm milk and yeast together until yeast has
dissolved.

Add sugar, melted butter, salt, egg, and two cups of flour.

Then add raisins. Beat to combine well.

Add enough more flour so that you can handle dough, knead for a few minutes, then let dough rest for a few minutes. Then knead until it is smooth and elastic, about ten minutes more, adding as little additional flour as possible.

Turn into a greased bowl, cover with plastic wrap, and refrigerate overnight.

In the morning:

As soon as you get up, remove dough from the refrigerator and let it warm, covered, for at least one-half hour.

Punch down dough and shape it roughly into buns. Crowd them in a 9-inch square pan so that they touch and let them rise until doubled, about an hour or less, depending on the warmth of the room.

Preheat oven to 400°F.

Bake buns about twenty minutes or until golden brown.

Brush with frosting, if desired, when buns have cooled a bit.

Makes about sixteen fat buns.

Scrambled Eggs Three Ways

These are scrambled eggs to please all. Use three skillets. Bacon flavors one batch, grated cheddar cheese flavors another, and the third is mixed with sour cream and chives or chopped scallions. Be sure to have cheese and sour cream at room temperature.

¼ pound bacon

1 dozen eggs, beaten with salt and pepper to taste and ¼ cup water

1 cup grated cheddar cheese

½ cup sour cream, mixed with ¼ cup chopped chives or scallions

9 tablespoons butter

While frying bacon, beat eggs with salt, pepper, and water.

Chop crisp bacon and set on paper to drain.

Melt three tablespoons butter in each of three skillets.

Pour one-third egg mixture into one skillet; add bacon.

Pour one-third egg mixture into another skillet; add grated cheese.

Mix sour cream and chives in remaining egg mixture, then pour into last skillet.

Cook eggs over very low heat, stirring each batch occasionally, until they are set.

Heap on a heated platter; garnish with extra crisped bacon, if desired, or parsley sprigs.

Serves six.

CHRISTMAS DINNER FOR THREE GENERATIONS

This dinner — usually served at midday — is the occasion for favorite family dishes, whatever they are, and for getting out everyone's favorite pickles, relishes, and preserves. Some Yankees supplement the turkey with a dish of chicken pie; others wouldn't feel properly festive without a dish of scalloped oysters. This is a substantial meal, intended to display the cook's expertise, the provider's generosity, and to linger in the memory as well as quite likely on the hips of the celebrants. A nostalgic but modern menu for a big family might include these dishes.

WINTER SQUASH SOUP

ROAST TURKEY WITH
OLD-FASHIONED BREAD STUFFING

FRESH CRANBERRY-ORANGE
RELISH (TWO WAYS)

RUTABAGA CASSEROLE

MAPLE-GLAZED PARSNIPS

CREAMED ONIONS

GREEN BEANS WITH CHESTNUTS

HARTWELL FARM CORN PUDDING

STEAMED CRANBERRY PUDDING
WITH HARD SAUCE
OR
BAKED CRANBERRY PUDDING
WITH HOT BUTTER SAUCE
OR
OLD-FASHIONED
CHRISTMAS PUDDING
AND MINCEMEAT PIE

Winter Squash Soup

This soup, rich and flavorful, reminds us of the summer's garden and the bounty of the squash harvest. It can be made with either water or chicken stock, and cream can be added at the end, if you like. A garnish of whipped cream dusted with ginger gives it a festive and elegant finish.

> ¼ pound sweet butter
>
> 2 large onions, diced
>
> 1 tablespoon minced fresh ginger
>
> 1 tablespoon good curry powder
>
> about 8 cups of cubed fresh winter
> squash (butternut, buttercup,
> Hubbard, or any other
> flavorful squash)
>
> 1 teaspoon salt
>
> ¼ teaspoon ground allspice
>
> 1 quart water or chicken stock
>
> cream if desired

Melt the butter, add diced onions, and saute with ginger until the onions are soft and transparent.

Add squash and water, and bring to a boil. Cook over moderate heat until the squash is very soft, about thirty minutes.

Strain the squash, puree in a food processor or food mill, return to liquid, and stir together.

Add salt to taste, allspice, and optional cream.

Serves six to eight.

Roast Turkey with Old-Fashioned Bread Stuffing

Roast your turkey any way you like – although recent reports indicate the high-temperature method is safest, and today's plump turkeys never seem to dry out – but when it comes to choosing a stuffing, the debate begins. Some Yankee cooks like to add apples, prunes, dried apricots, or nuts at Christmastime, but there is much to be said for the classic New England bread stuffing, lightly seasoned, which absorbs the bird's own juices and is served forth moist and crumbly at the same time. Cook the turkey until tender and leg juices run clear, about twenty minutes to the pound.

> 8 to 10 cups bread, torn into small pieces
>
> 2 cups onions, chopped fine
>
> 3 stalks celery, chopped fine
>
> ½ cup minced parsley
>
> 2 tablespoons poultry seasoning or
>
> > 1 tablespoon sage and 1 tablespoon
> >
> > mixed thyme and marjoram
>
> 1 tablespoon salt
>
> 1 teaspoon black pepper
>
> 1 beaten egg
>
> enough stock or milk to moisten

Mix all ingredients in a large bowl and stuff the turkey's cavity, lightly, allowing room for stuffing to swell.

Makes enough stuffing for a twelve- to sixteen-pound turkey.

Fresh Cranberry-Orange Relish

This fresh-tasting alternative for the usual cranberry sauce has become a staple on holiday tables. Best made in a meat grinder or food processor.

> 3 cups cranberries
>
> 1 medium orange
>
> about 1 cup sugar

Seed the orange and grind it with the cranberries. Add sugar to taste.

Makes about three cups.

Patty's Christmas Relish

Patty Withington's family likes this variation. She likes to garnish it with sliced kiwi fruit and carrot flowers.

> 1 package fresh cranberries
>
> (about 3 cups)
>
> juice of 2 oranges
>
> ¾ cup honey or to taste
>
> 2 cups coconut

Wash cranberries.

Process cranberries with orange juice.

Stir in honey and coconut.

Garnish, chill, and serve.

Makes about four cups.

Rutabaga Casserole

A pudding of rutabagas, or yellow turnips, is a traditional staple at the New Englander's Christmas dinner. Even people who think they don't like turnip like this dish.

6 cups peeled and diced rutabaga

½ cup fine bread crumbs

½ cup light cream

3 eggs

½ teaspoon nutmeg

1 teaspoon salt

¼ cup butter

Cook rutabagas in salted water to cover until they are soft, about twenty to thirty minutes. Drain and mash.

Mix bread crumbs and cream in large bowl.

Beat eggs, add spices.

Combine all ingredients and mix well.

Pour into a well-buttered baking dish and bake in a 350°F oven for about one hour.

Serves six to eight.

Maple-Glazed Parsnips

1½ to 2 pounds parsnips

3 tablespoons butter

¼ cup maple syrup

⅓ cup apple cider

½ teaspoon salt

Peel parsnips, cook in salted water until tender. Drain.

Arrange parsnips in a baking dish.

Mix butter, syrup, cider, and salt, and pour over parsnips.

Bake about one-half hour in 375°F oven, basting frequently, or until parsnips are brown and glazed.

Serves eight.

Creamed Onions

Tiny, thin-skinned, white onions, sometimes called silverskins, are a traditional favorite at Christmastime.

3 to 4 cups small, white onions

2 tablespoons butter

2 tablespoons flour

1 to 1½ cups light cream

1 teaspoon salt

pinch of nutmeg

¼ cup buttered bread crumbs

Cook peeled onions in salted water to cover until just tender.

Make a thin cream sauce; melt butter, mix in flour, cream, and seasonings, stirring well to avoid lumps.

Arrange onions in buttered baking dish and pour sauce over them. Sprinkle buttered bread crumbs on top.

Bake in 350°F oven until heated through and crumbs are brown.

Serves six to eight.

Green Beans
with Chestnuts

Tasty and elegant.

> 2 pounds green beans
>
> ⅔ cup cooked chestnuts
>
> ½ cup butter

Steam about one-half pound shelled chestnuts forty-five

minutes or use canned chestnuts. Chop roughly.

Saute chestnuts in butter.

Cook beans until just tender.

Toss beans and chestnuts together and season with salt

and pepper.

Serves eight.

Hartwell Farm
Corn Pudding

*A Kendall family favorite. At that Massachusetts
family's table, there is never a bit of this easy
pudding left when it's time for dessert.*

> 2 cups creamed corn
>
> 1 cup dry bread crumbs
>
> 1 cup milk
>
> 2 tablespoons chopped green pepper
>
> 4 ounces sliced cheddar cheese
>
> 4 strips cooked bacon
>
> salt and pepper to taste

Combine corn, crumbs, milk, and green pepper. Season to

taste with salt and pepper.

Pour into deep baking dish about 10 x 6-inches.

Arrange alternating strips of cheese and bacon across

the top.

Bake in 350°F oven one to one and a half hours.

Serves six to eight.

Aunt Amy's
Steamed Cranberry
Pudding

*Christmas dinner at Brookside Farm in Westminster,
Massachusetts, is always followed by Aunt Amy's
special steamed pudding with fluffy hard sauce. Aunt
Amy's parents used to bring the cranberries up from
Cape Cod where they were raised by Finnish
farmers in Centerville. The cook recommends
doubling the recipe for hard sauce.*

> 1 cup fresh cranberries, halved
>
> 1 cup crushed canned pineapple, drained
>
> ½ cup roughly chopped walnuts
>
> ½ cup light molasses
>
> 1½ cups flour
>
> ½ teaspoon salt
>
> 1 teaspoon baking soda
>
> ¼ teaspoon cinnamon
>
> ¼ teaspoon ground cloves
>
> ¼ teaspoon nutmeg

Combine fruits, nuts, and molasses. Add sifted dry
ingredients and mix well. Fill greased one-quart
mold about two-thirds full. Cover tightly. Place mold
on a rack in a kettle with boiling water reaching
halfway up the mold and steam two hours.

Garnish with almonds or pecan halves, if desired.

Unmold and serve with Fluffy Hard Sauce.

This pudding can be made ahead of time and reheated,
well-wrapped, in a 325°F oven.

Serves ten or more.

Fluffy Hard Sauce

1 cup butter

2 cups sifted confectioners' sugar

1 cup heavy cream

1 teaspoon vanilla

Thoroughly cream butter and sugar. Beat in cream
and vanilla.

Aunt Amy's Baked Cranberry Pudding

This is a family favorite that's easier and quicker to
make than Steamed Cranberry Pudding—and
honestly, aren't there times when a shortcut is
imperative? But the hot butter sauce "transports it
into heavenly delight," according to my aunt. Try it.

2 cups flour

1 cup sugar

2½ teaspoons baking powder

¼ teaspoon salt

3 tablespoons melted butter or margarine

⅔ cup milk

1 egg

1½ cups cranberries, ground

Sift dry ingredients. Add butter or margarine, milk, and
egg. Beat two minutes. Stir in cranberries.

Bake in 8-inch square pan in 350°F oven for forty
minutes.

Serve with Hot Butter Sauce.

Serves eight.

Hot Butter Sauce

½ cup butter

1 cup sugar

¾ cup milk or light cream

Melt butter. Add sugar and cream, mix well.

Cook five minutes, stirring occasionally.

Serve hot.

Old-Fashioned Christmas Pudding

For New Englanders who cling to Old English tradition, there are only two possible desserts at Christmas dinner: mince pie or the sort of steamed pudding immortalized by Charles Dickens in A Christmas Carol. Many traditions attend the pudding—that it must be stirred (clockwise, while making a wish) by everyone in the household, that of baking coins and other tokens inside it to portend fortune for the year to come. This recipe has been used continuously for at least a hundred years by the Nelson family of Boston and New Hampshire. Butter may be substituted for the traditional suet, if you prefer. Serve with the same Fluffy Hard Sauce used for Cranberry Steamed Pudding, above. Presented in shiny molds, steamed puddings make fine gifts; they are easily reheated.

> 2½ cups flour
>
> 1 teaspoon soda
>
> ½ teaspoon salt
>
> 2 teaspoons cinnamon
>
> 1 teaspoon nutmeg
>
> 1 teaspoon cloves
>
> 1 cup chopped suet or butter
>
> 1 cup raisins
>
> 1 cup chopped dates
>
> 1 cup chopped nuts
>
> 2 eggs, beaten
>
> 1 cup milk or sour milk
>
> 1 cup molasses

Sift dry ingredients.

Cut in suet or butter as for pastry.

Add fruit and nuts.

Combine beaten eggs, milk, and molasses and add gradually to flour mixture.

Pour into a well-greased pudding mold and set in a kettle of water. Steam three hours. Unmold.

To serve the pudding flaming, unmold it on a flameproof or metal platter; soak small sugar cubes in brandy or lemon extract and set them on fire as the pudding is served.

Serves eight to ten.

Mincemeat Pie

Make a pie using plain pastry filled with either traditional mincemeat or green tomato mincemeat. Fresh apple, additional raisins, or nuts may be added to mincemeat just before baking, and those who like may flavor the filling with brandy.

Bake mincemeat pie in 400°F oven about one hour.

CRAFTS

Christmas Crafts

All items that are made by hand have a special mystique about them. They represent to us a bond with their maker, known or unknown. It gives us respect, if not love for the effort that was put forth. Whenever we make something with our hands, no matter how refined or crude, we give of ourselves.

Author Unknown

Christmas is a time of giving, and what better gift to give than one you've made yourself. Folk crafts are a strong part of the Yankee tradition. America's earliest settlers often lacked the resources to obtain what they coveted. But this lack served as a catalyst for resourcefulness, for more important than tangible goods, these folks used their individual talents and ideas that unleashed a spirit of creativity. Unencumbered by ideas of what they could not do, they created crafts for the pure joy of creating.

In that tradition, these crafts were designed for those wanting to rediscover that joy and satisfaction of working with one's hands and the giving of a gift created by oneself. For every person who makes one of these Christmas projects, there will likely be at least a dozen who will enjoy receiving or just looking at it.

Don't be overcautious with perfection. Just enjoy creating and giving these crafts in the spirit of Christmas.

Carole Yeager

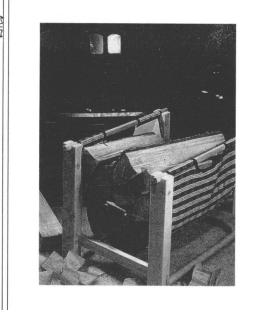

Log Carrier And Stand

It has been said that a man who builds a fire is warmed twice by the wood, once when he gathers it and again when it's burned. Make the gathering an easier task by giving the keeper of your hearth this sturdy log carrier and stand. Made from a classic plaid fabric (as pictured) or one coordinated to your home, this practical gift becomes an admired decorative accessory as well.

SUPPLIES

Carrier:

19"x 41" piece of heavy cotton fabric

19"x 41" piece of canvas or cotton duck (lining)

one package (3 yards) of ½" single-fold bias tape

thread to match

two 23" lengths of ¾" dowel

stain or clear varnish

1 felt square

Stand:

four 20″ lengths of 2″x 3″ pine (uprights)

two 18″ lengths of 1″x 2″ pine (rails)

two 21¾″ lengths of 1″ dowel

eight 1″ #8 flat-head wood screws

four 1¼″ #12 round-head brass wood screws

MAKING THE CARRIER

1. Make a paper pattern for the handle cut-out. Right sides facing, pin canvas and fabric together. Pin the handle pattern to the center (9½″) of the short end of fabric. Cut around the pattern through both layers. Repeat at the other end.

2. Sew fabric and canvas together ⅜″ from the straight edge of the handle side. (Do not stitch the handle cut-out. Repeat at the other end. Turn carrier right side out and press seam. Encase both side edges and handle cut-outs with bias tape and stitch.

3. To make a sleeve for the wood handles, fold the handle edge down 1½″, press, and sew in place as close to the edge as possible. To reinforce, sew over the previous stitching.

4. Stain or varnish both dowel pieces the same color as you will be using for the stand, and set aside to dry. When dry, insert dowels through hemmed edges.

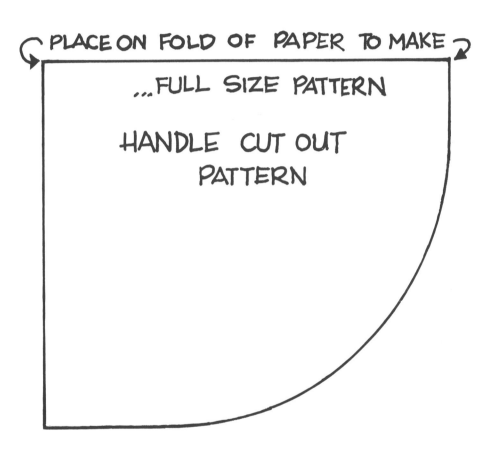

PLACE ON FOLD OF PAPER TO MAKE

...FULL SIZE PATTERN

HANDLE CUT OUT
PATTERN

MAKING THE STAND

1. From a six- or seven-foot length of 2"x 3" pine, cut four lengths about 20" long. On each piece, place a centered mark at a distance of 17¾" from one squared end, and a squared line next to it at a distance of 18". Use a ¾" spade bit, drill a hole through the board at the

17¾″ mark. Now cut the board at the line. At the other end of each piece, place a centered mark 2½″ from the end. Using a ¼″ bit, drill a hole to a depth of approximately ½″. To mark the placement of the dowel, turn the board over to the opposite side and place a mark at the same location. Using a 1″ spade bit, drill a hole at this mark to a depth of precisely 1″. Use care to keep the drill perpendicular to the board. Repeat for all four boards. Next, make the end rail slots. From the end and side with the 1″ hole, draw two squared lines: one at 3½″ and the other at 5″. Extend these lines ¾″ across each edge of the board. On each edge, draw a centered line between these two lines. Remove this piece (¾″ x 1½″ x 2½″) with a saw to form the rail slot. Repeat until all four have been cut.

2. For the rails, cut two 18″ lengths of 1″x 2″ (actually 1½″) pine, squared ends.

3. To assemble, place one 1″x 2″ board in the channels cut in the uprights, ends flush with the side. Using a #8 countersink bit, drill screw holes through the rails into the uprights at the locations shown. Fasten the rails to the uprights using four 1″ #8 flat-head wood screws, slightly countersunk. Assemble the other end of the stand in the same manner. Cut two lengths of 1″ dowel 21¾″. (So the uprights stand straight, be

certain that these dowels have squared ends.) Find the center of each end and drill four ⁵⁄₃₂″ pilot holes 1″ deep. Place dowels in the holes of the uprights and attach, using four 1¼″ #12 brass round-head wood screws.

4. Stain or varnish. To protect your floor from scratches, glue felt to the bottom of each leg. For easy storage, remove the four brass screws to release the dowels from the uprights.

Calico

Cat

Doorstop

This charmer will stop passersby as well as your door with its lifelike stance and stare. When not holding a door, it looks equally disarming tucked among your houseplants or on a shelf or windowsill.

SUPPLIES

12″ length of 1″x 10″ pine

4″ length of 2″x 2″ pine

wood sealer (optional)

sandpaper, tack cloth

tracing and graphite paper

wood glue

black, white, ivory, rust, avocado, and yellow acrylic paints

assorted artist's brushes (three)

clear satin finish varnish (optional)

1. Transfer cat pattern and painting guide lines to tracing paper. Slip graphite paper between the wood and pattern and transfer body outline to the wood; cut with a band or jig saw. Cut stopper from 2″ x 2″ pine. Sand and seal cat. Let dry, sand again lightly (sealer tends to raise the grain), and wipe with a tack cloth to remove grit. Paint the stopper and the back of the cat black. Since glue will not adhere as well to a painted surface, leave those portions of the stopper and back that will be joined unpainted.

2. Transfer painting guidelines to the wood. You will be painting in layers: base-coating, followed by dry-brushing, and, lastly, all detail painting. Let each coat dry thoroughly before going to the next.

Base-coating: Using the photo and pattern as a guide, paint the hind quarters, between legs, parts of the face and head, and the edges (bordering on black areas) black. Paint the chest, legs, and inside the ears ivory. Paint the face white with rust markings. Mix a very transparent rust wash and shade below the mouth, chin, and neckline, above the paws and inside each ear.

Dry-brushing: Dry-brushing, done with a slightly splayed natural bristle brush (stencil brush will do), is used to give the fur a wispy, hairlike appearance, to soften the edges, and to add depth to the base-coated areas.

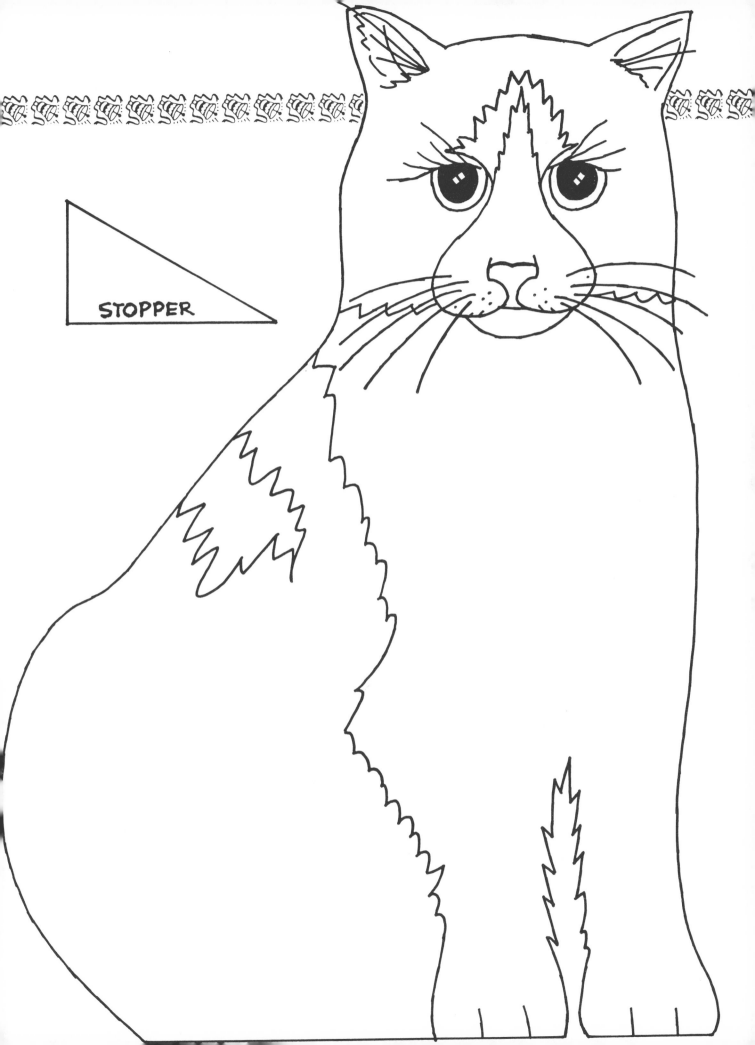

STOPPER

Do not paint opaquely; the base color should show through. Dip your brush into the white paint and stroke it across a paper towel to remove excess paint. Bristles should be fairly dry. Using quick, light, wispy strokes, paint hairs on the chest and leg areas, the chin, and muzzle. With the splayed brush dipped in rust use the same technique to paint markings on the back and a few small patches randomly around the body. *Details:* (Use a fine brush.) Mix rust with ivory and paint the nose. Paint the entire eye avocado green; then before the paint is completely dry, blend yellow into the green from the bottom up to about the middle of the eye. Blend colors so there is no obvious demarcation line. Let dry. Paint the pupils black and highlight each with a tiny fleck of white. Thin black slightly with water so it will flow smoothly and paint whiskers (add a few white ones for variety), define toes, and add fine hairs in the ears. Outline the eyes, mouth, and the bottom of the nose with thinned black. Add black and white lashes.

3. Center and glue the stopper to the back. Optional: Finish with a coat of clear varnish.

Corn Husk Santa

Lovingly fashioned from all-natural materials, this homespun Santa has the look of a treasured keepsake from Christmas past. Make him from prepackaged husks (available in craft stores) or use those from your own garden. Before using those from your garden, spread them between two window screens and dry thoroughly in the sun.

SUPPLIES

24 large corn husks

powdered red fabric dye

florist's thin wire

natural wool or mock wool fiber

cotton balls

6″ pipe cleaner

purchased miniature toys and tree

white craft glue

white thread

pink and blue colored pencils

paper towels

scissors

1. Make a dye bath by mixing one package of powdered dye with two quarts of very hot water. Immerse about eight large husks in the dye. Soak husks for about fifteen minutes (color will lighten when dry). When the desired color is reached, rinse husks under cold water, blot dry on paper towels, and set them aside. Note: Keep the husks between the damp towels since they cannot be worked with when dry.

2. For head, arms, and body, soak about sixteen husks in warm water until pliable (about ten minutes), then blot on a towel.

For the head, choose two smooth, fine-grained husks and tie them together at the narrow end with wire. Invert the husks (keeping the tied ends to the inside), fan out each section and wrap the husks smoothly around a 1″ ball made from seven or eight cotton balls or styrofoam. Twist wire tightly around the husks just under the ball, leaving excess husks extended (Fig. 1).

For arms, tightly roll a 6″ pipe cleaner in a 2″ x 8″ husk. Form

FIG 2

FIG 1

FIG 3

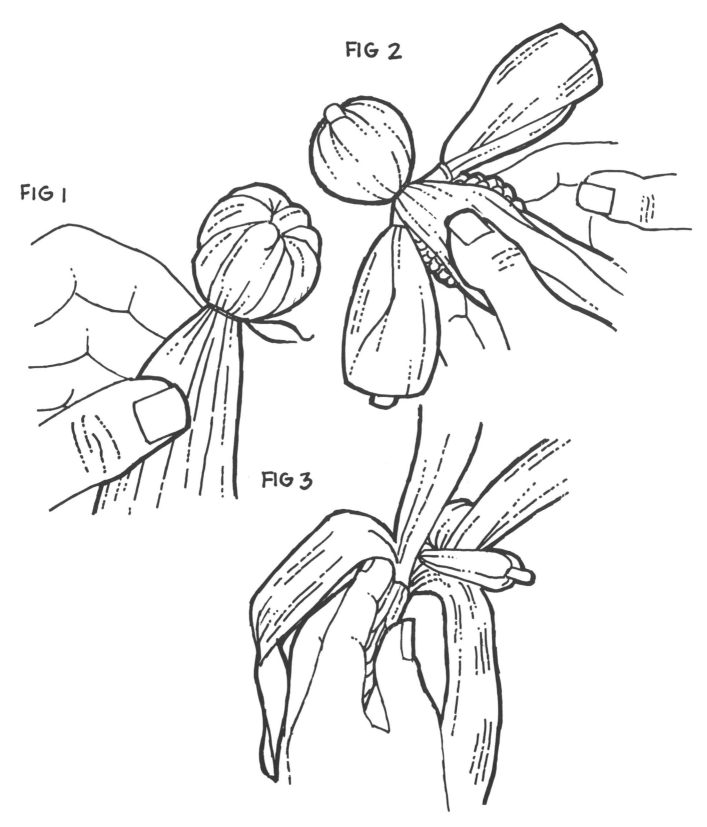

hands by bending the excess husk at each end and securing it at the "wrist" with wire. For sleeves, cut one large dyed husk in half (across the width) and tie the end of one half tightly at each wrist. Invert the sleeve, shaping it over the arm so there are no gaps and wire the sleeve to the center. Repeat on the other side.

For the body, slide the completed arms between the husks extending below the head; form the chest by stuffing this portion with cotton balls (Fig. 2). Tie at the waist with wire.

For a full skirt, choose ten to twelve uniformly sized undyed husks. Arrange the narrow ends of the husks evenly around the waist, wide ends extending over the head (Fig. 3). Tie at the waist with wire. Fold the husks down to form a skirt, trim evenly along the bottom edge, then wrap wire loosely around the edge and leave in place until dry (overnight). When dry, remove this loosely wrapped wire.

For the robe, choose three large dyed husks (or six small). With the wide ends of the husks extending over the head, place the narrow end of one on each side of the head (front) and one at the back of the head; wire them all in place tightly around the neck. Fold the husks down and wrap a wire loosely around the waist until dry. Apply a line of glue down the front and along the bottom edge of the robe. Press wool in

place. (For a more natural look, pull the wool apart into long strips rather than cut it.) Glue wool in place on each sleeve.

Finish with colored pencils, coloring the cheeks and mouth area pink and drawing blue dots for eyes. Glue beard and hair in place. For a hat, cut a small (about 4"x 4") dyed husk and glue one edge in place around the head, let dry. Twist the other end, tie with wire. Trim with wool. Bend the end and glue in place. For a mustache, twist a small piece of wool in the center, tie with white thread, and glue in place. For a sack, wire two husks together at one end, turn inside out, stuff lightly with cotton balls, then tie loosely at the top with wire; when dry, glue on a thin strip of husk for a handle. Glue the sack in place on his shoulder and accent with small toys or packages (made from squares of folded husks). Tie a thin strip of husk or raffia around his waist and glue a small evergreen or twig staff in his hand. Shape glasses by twisting wire around a small pencil. Spray wool with hairspray to keep in place.

Little Red Riding Hood Dolls

Here's the whole cast of characters from one of childhood's all-time favorite fairy tales. Little Red Riding Hood looks enchanting in her red cape, calico dress, and basket brimming with treats. What child wouldn't be surprised and delighted to discover the cunning wolf and kindly grandmother both fashioned into one topsy-turvy doll? With a flip of the skirt, one appears while the other makes a quick getaway! Make all three dolls, the single Red Riding Hood and the duplex wolf/grandma, from basically the same pattern pieces, and really bring this story to life for a special child in your life.

SUPPLIES

Little Red Riding Hood:

½ yard bleached muslin (45″ width) (body, bloomers, apron)

¼ yard calico fabric (45″) (dress)

10″x 20″ red felt (cape)

20″ of ⅜″ red ribbon (cape)

30″ of ⅜″ white ribbon (apron)

14″ of ⅛″ ribbon (braids)

1½ yards ¾″ pregathered lace

tracing or tissue paper

dressmakers' carbon paper

brown yarn

peach, white, brown, green, black, and rose acrylic paints

brushes

polyester fiberfill

small basket

small piece of velcro

6½″ length of ¼″ elastic

1. Make tracing or tissue paper patterns.
2. For the body, cut body, arms, and legs from muslin, adding ¼″
seam allowance to each piece. With right sides pinned together, sew the
body, leaving arm openings and bottom edge open. Clip curves, turn right
side out, and press the ¼″ seam allowance at each opening to the
inside. Sew arms and legs, leaving the straight edges open. Clip curves

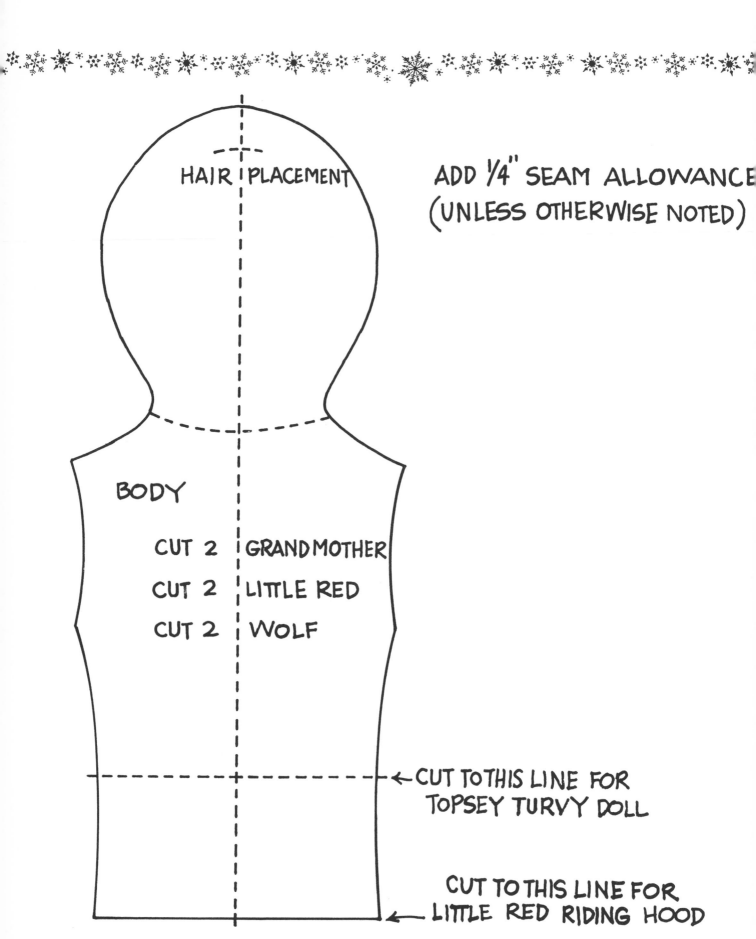

HAIR | PLACEMENT

ADD ¼" SEAM ALLOWANCE
(UNLESS OTHERWISE NOTED)

BODY

CUT 2 | GRANDMOTHER

CUT 2 | LITTLE RED

CUT 2 | WOLF

← CUT TO THIS LINE FOR
TOPSEY TURVY DOLL

CUT TO THIS LINE FOR
← LITTLE RED RIDING HOOD

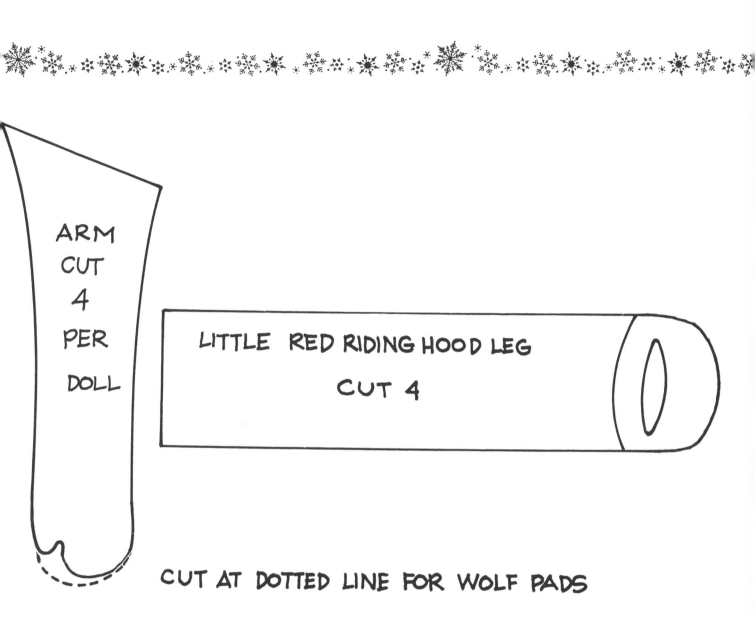

ARM

CUT

4

PER

DOLL

LITTLE RED RIDING HOOD LEG

CUT 4

CUT AT DOTTED LINE FOR WOLF PADS

and turn right side out. Stuff half of each arm with fiberfill, stop, and stitch across the arm. Finish stuffing each arm, then stitch openings closed. Stuff legs firmly and stitch ends closed. Insert arms into body opening, stitch in place. Stuff body firmly, insert legs into body, stitch in place. Paint head, arms, and legs peach. Let dry. Paint shoes black. Paint face with a fine brush, referring to pattern for colors.

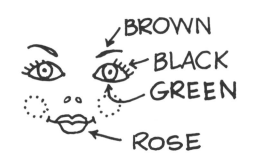

BROWN
BLACK
GREEN

ROSE

LITTLE RED RIDING
HOOD'S FACE

3. For the hair, cut a piece of cardboard 2½" wide by 14" long. Wrap brown yarn around cardboard about twenty times, distributing it evenly across the 2½" width. Carefully remove yarn and lay it flat, keeping loops evenly distributed. Machine stitch through the center of the yarn several times (Fig. 1). Cut loops open at each end. Center yarn on

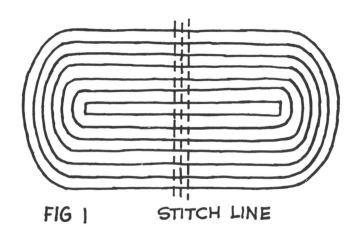

FIG 1   STITCH LINE

head, positioning it on forehead at placement line. Tack to head along stitch line. Divide yarn, trim ends evenly, and tack to the head at the

hairline, about ear level. Braid. Tie tightly at each end with thread and finish with a bow.

4. Cut four pieces for bloomers. Right sides together, sew center seam of two pieces to make front. Clip curves, press. Repeat steps to make back. Right sides together, sew front to back at one side seam. Press hem of leg up ¼″ and topstitch thin lace to the edge. Repeat this step on the other leg. With right sides together, sew inside leg seam, clip curves. Press raw edges under at the waist. Stitch a 6½″ length of ¼″ elastic to the waist, stretching as you sew. Clip off excess 1″ of elastic. Turn right side out.

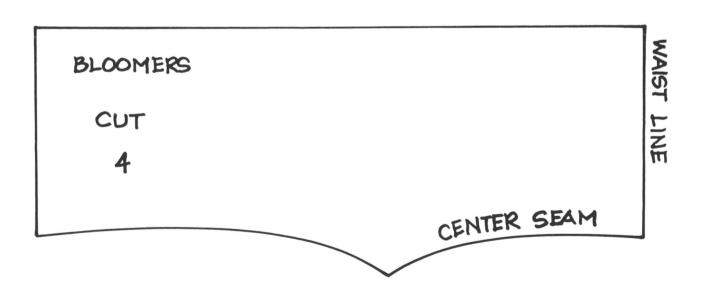

5. Cut one bodice front and two bodice back pieces (transfer dots) from calico fabric. Cut two sleeves. Stitch front to back at shoulder seams.

DRESS SLEEVE
CUT 2 PER DOLL

PLACE ON FOLD

NO SEAM ALLOWANCE
IS NECESSARY

BODICE BIB
CUT 2
PLACE ON FOLD

BODICE
CUT 1 FOR THE FRONT
AND 2 FOR THE BACK

PLACE ON FOLD

Right sides together, pin sleeves to bodice, baste, easing fabric to fit between dots. Stitch. Clip curves and press. Turn and press ¼" fabric under on each sleeve and around the neck; trim with lace. With right sides together, stitch underarm seams. Clip and trim seams, turn right side out. Sew decorative buttons down the front, if desired.

6. Cut a strip of calico fabric 6" wide by 22" long for the skirt. Press bottom edge of skirt under ¼" and trim with lace. Gather skirt by sewing with large machine stitches ⅛" from the top edge. Pull thread until the gathered edge measures about 7½". Spread gathering

evenly, leaving ¼" on each end ungathered. With right sides together, pin the bodice to the gathered skirt edge, stitch across. Stitch back seam of skirt together. Put dress on doll and slipstitch bodice opening closed.

7. Cut a 5½" wide by 12" long piece of muslin for the apron. Press side and bottom edges under ⅛" twice. Stitch. Trim apron with lace, decorative ribbon, or rickrack. Gather top edge by sewing with large machine stitches ⅛" from the edge. Pull thread until the gathered edge measures 4½". Spread gathers evenly. Center and topstitch a 30" length of ribbon to the edge.

8. For the cape, fold felt piece to form a 10"x 10" square. Using the

FIG 2 CAPE

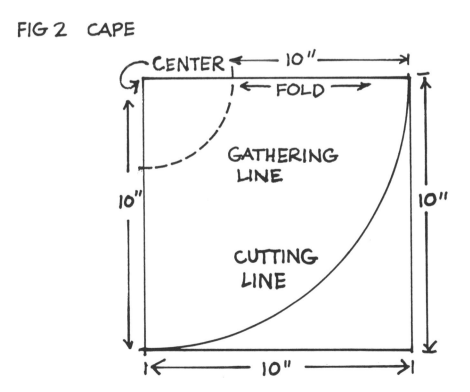

folded corner as a center point, draw an arc with a 10″ radius. Cut. From the same center point, draw an arc with a 4″ radius. When gathered, this will form the hood (Fig. 2). Sew a loose basting stitch over this line. Pull the thread until the gathering measures 4″. Spread gathering evenly, leaving ¼″ on each end ungathered. Center 20″ red ribbon over the gathering on the right side of the cape and stitch in place.

9. To finish, sew a small piece of velcro to each hand. Glue a scrap of fabric to the inside of the basket and fill with miniature treats.

SUPPLIES

Topsy-turvy Doll:

⅓ yard bleached muslin (45″ width) for body, dress bib, and nightcap lining

½ yard cotton print fabric

2 yards ¾″ pre-gathered lace

12″ of ¼″ elastic

white yarn

Calico Cat Doorstop

Corn Husk Santa

Little Red Riding Hood Dolls

Twig Bed

Orange Pomanders

Wreath and Garland

small piece medium-weight wire (glasses)

peach, brown, white, black, rose, blue, and gold acrylic paints

brushes

polyester fiberfill

tissue or tracing paper

dressmaker's carbon paper

small piece fusable interfacing

1. Make tissue paper patterns. Cut all body pieces from white muslin, adding ¼″ seam allowance to each piece.

Grandma:

2. Right sides together, stitch body, leaving arm openings and bottom edge open. Clip seams, turn right side out, and press ¼″ seam allowance at the arms and bottom to the inside. Right sides together, sew arms, leaving straight edge open. Turn right side out, press. Stuff half of each arm with fiberfill, stitch across arm, then continue to stuff to the ends. Stitch opening closed, without turning the seam allowance to the inside. Insert arms into body (thumbs up) and stitch in place. Stuff body firmly.

Paint head, neck, and arms peach. Allow to dry. Paint face details, referring to pattern. Outline features with a very thin line of brown.

GRANDMOTHER'S FACE

3. For the hair, cut a piece of cardboard 2½" wide by 6" long. Wrap white yarn around cardboard about thirty times, distributing it evenly. Carefully remove yarn from the cardboard and cut in half at one end. Machine stitch through the middle several times. Center hair on head (overlapping on the forehead to the hair placement line) and tack in place on the stitch line. Pull the hair to the back of the neck, evenly distributing it over the head. Trim ends. Tack in place around the base of the neck. Tie at the back with a ribbon.

Wolf:

4. Right sides together, stitch body, leaving arm, neck, and bottom edge open. Turn right side out, clip curves, and press ¼" seam allowance on the arm and neck openings to the inside. Stitch arms leaving the straight

edges open. Turn right sides out, press. Stuff half of each arm with fiberfill, stitch across, then continue to stuff to the ends. Stitch openings closed on the seam allowance. (Do not turn the ¼″ to the inside.) Insert arms into body and stitch in place.

5. Sew ears, turn right side out, press. Right sides together, sew head side pieces from the neck edge to point A, and from the neck edge to point B. Cut ear slit open on the head pieces. On the right side of the

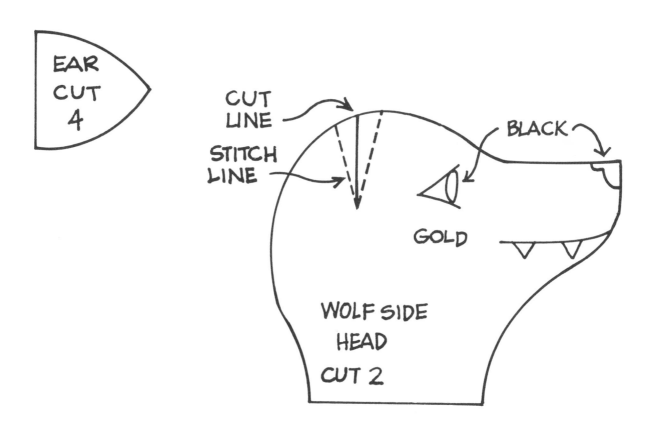

head piece, insert an ear (facing the nose) into each slit, cup ear slightly to fit and stitch in place, catching all raw edges in the seam (Fig. 3).

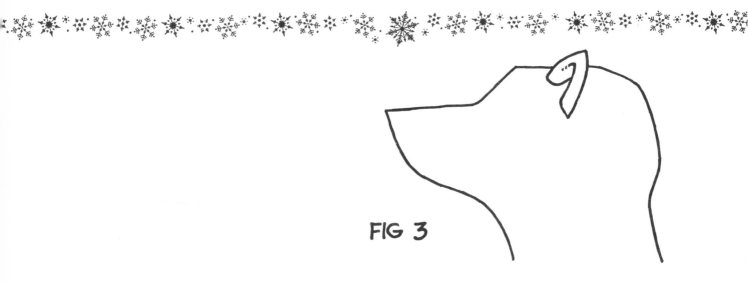

FIG 3

Pin gusset to head side pieces, matching dots. Baste, easing to fit. Stitch, being careful not to catch the ears in the seam. Trim seams, clip curves, and turn right side out. Stuff firmly, shaping head as you stuff.

PLACE ON FOLD

CUT 1

WOLF HEAD GUSSET

6. Stuff the body loosely and insert the bottom edge of the wolf body into the bottom edge of the grandmother's body. Pin in place. Hand stitch the bodies together. Stuff the body firmly up to the neck. Insert head into the body (facing the same direction as the grandmother's face), pin in place, and slipstitch seam closed.

7. Mix black with white paint for gray. Paint wolf's head and arms gray. Paint inside the ears and the muzzle a lighter shade of gray.

Let dry. Paint details. (Refer to pattern for colors.) Outline mouth and eyes black.

8. To make the bodice for the wolf and grandmother's dress, follow Step 5 bodice directions under Little Red Riding Hood. Note: Cut two bibs from muslin and two from fusable interfacing. Fuse interfacing to bibs. Pin bibs to the center of the bodice fronts, trim with lace, and sew. Add a ribbon bow at the neckline.

9. Cut two strips of fabric for the skirt, each 7" wide by 28" long. Cut a 27½" length of lace trim. Place the straight edge of the lace along the right side edge of one skirt, starting it ¼" from the end. Place the other skirt over this piece, right sides together, matching edges. Stitch skirts' bottoms together ¼" from the edge. Turn right sides out, press. Gather each skirt piece (separately) by running a loose machine stitch ⅛" from the edge. Pull the thread until the gathered edge measures about 7½". Spread gathering evenly, leaving ¼" on each side ungathered. Right sides together, pin skirts to bodice, stitch. Right sides together, match skirt at the waistline, hem, and other waistline. Stitch back skirt seam, using one continuous seam from one waistline to the other. Turn right side out. Topstitch close to the skirt edge. Dress the doll and hand stitch bodices closed.

10. Cut two pieces from muslin (lining) and two from cotton print for the two nightcaps. Right sides together, pin lining to top. Stitch, leaving a

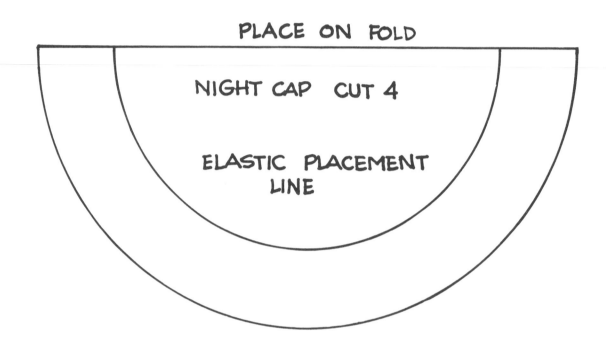

PLACE ON FOLD

NIGHT CAP   CUT 4

ELASTIC PLACEMENT
LINE

1½″ opening for turning. Clip curves, turn right side out. Press, turning in seam allowance at opening. Topstitch close to the edge. Cut 6″ piece of ¼″ elastic per cap. Sew elastic to the inside of the cap on the placement line, stretching elastic tightly as you sew. Cut off excess elastic. Place cap on wolf's head, cut small slits for the ear to protrude (push raw edges to the inside), and tack in place. Tack other cap to grandmother's head. Bend a small piece of wire into the shape of glasses (see diagram). Stitch to grandmother's face.

GLASSES

Twig Bed

Although this rustic twig bed looks as though it was found in a cottage nestled deep in the Black Forest, it's much more accessible than that. A stroll through the woods can provide you with just what you need for the frame, while the rope mattress is made from jute twine. So you have a better selection of pieces to work with, gather more branches than you will actually need. Try to choose the same kind of wood for all pieces but the spindles. (They can be made from cuttings left over after you have pruned a tree or large shrub.) For an interesting-looking headboard, look for a branch with an attractive bend.

SUPPLIES

7' of straight ¾" to 1" diameter saplings (branches)

1' of bent ¾" diameter sapling (branches), suitable for the top of the headboard

5' of ⁵⁄₁₆" straight saplings (twigs) for head and foot board spindles

15′ of thin jute twine

large needle

twelve 1½″ #6 round-head wood screws

wood glue

ten ⅝″ wire nails

From the ¾″-1″ diameter branch, cut:

    two 9″ lengths (head posts)

    two 6″ lengths (foot posts)

    two 14″ lengths (side rails)

    two 8″ lengths (head and foot rails)

    one 10″ length (the top of the foot)

    one 10″ length of bent wood for the top of the headboard

1. *Posts* Drill one ⁵⁄₆₄″ hole through the center of each post 4″ from the bottom end. Rotate the pieces ninety degrees and drill a ⁵⁄₆₄″ hole through the center 3½″ from the same end of each post.

2. *Side rails* Make holes for weaving the twine by drilling twelve ⁵⁄₆₄″ holes through the center of each rail spacing each hole one inch apart (starting 1½″ from both ends). To facilitate easier weaving, open the

holes completely by drilling through each previously drilled hole from the other side.

3. *Head/foot bottom rails* For spindle placement, using a 5⁄64″ drill bit, drill five pilot holes spaced 1¼″ apart, spaced 1½″ from each end, through the center of each piece. Open the pilot holes by redrilling each with a 3⁄8″ bit.

Head/foot top pieces Center the bottom rail next to the corresponding top, and using the bottom rails as a guide, mark corresponding holes on the underside of the top pieces. With the 5⁄64″ bit, drill pilot holes HALFWAY through and redrill each (halfway through) with a 3⁄8″ bit. For attachment to the post, drill a 5⁄64″ hole about ¾″ from the ends on each piece.

4. *Frame* Using 1½″ screws, attach the side rails to the posts at the 4″ holes, the head and foot bottom rails to the posts at the 3½″ holes. The screws should be aligned with the center (heartwood) of each rail. Tighten screws firmly. Center the top pieces on the appropriate posts. Now mark and cut the top pieces so they are flush with the posts. Shave the underside of the head piece ends so it rests evenly when screwed to the posts. Attach the top pieces to the top of each post.

5. *Spindles* Turn the bed upside down. Cut ten 5⁄16″ twigs in various

lengths from 4″ to 8″. (The finished lengths are determined by sliding the piece through the bottom rail holes until seated in the corresponding hole in the top rail and marking at the lower side of the bottom rail.) After cutting the spindles to the proper length, put a small drop of wood glue into each top piece hole and insert spindles. Let dry. Turn bed right side up. To secure spindles in place, drive a ⅝″ wire nail through the inside bottom rail into each spindle.

6. *Twine* Thread a large needle with twine. Beginning at one corner, push the needle through a hole in the side rail, wrap the twine around the rail once, and knot the end to secure it. Begin weaving the twine back and forth across the sides, pulling it taut, until you have all holes filled. When completed, wrap the twine around the rail and knot the end.

Noah's Ark

This classic toy is as loved today as it was years ago when it was given as a "Sunday toy" meant to be played with quietly on a Sabbath afternoon. This sturdy ark comes with ten pairs of animals, but don't stop there. Start a family tradition by adding a new set to the menagerie each Christmas. When it's not being played with, just lift the cabin and store all the animals safely below deck.

SUPPLIES

4' of 1"x 6" pine (bottom & deck)

1' of 1"x 4" pine (cabin ends)

3' of ½"x 6" pine (figures)

9" of clear 2"x 6" pine or fir—not pressure treated! (deck spacer)

1'x 3' piece of ⅛" luan plywood (sides)

pine lattice (¼" thickness):

    10½" of 1⅝" width (ramp)

Supplies continued on the following page

38″ of 3⅝″ width (cabin sides & one-half roof)

13″ of 5¼″ width (bow/stern pieces & one-half roof)

¾″ wire brads

1″ paneling nails

wood putty

wood glue

assorted acrylic paints and brushes

yarn or sisal twine for tails

CONSTRUCTION OF ARK

1. *Ark Bottom* Draw end to end centerlines on both sides of a 22″ length of 1″x 6″. Trace pattern piece A onto the wood on the centerline at one end. Measure along the centerline from the point of this tracing a distance of 20⁷⁄₁₆″ and mark. Reverse the pattern, align the point of it on this mark, and trace onto the wood. Make sure that these tracing lines avoid any knots. Set the saw blade angle adjustment (either saber or band) to fifteen degrees. Cut this piece with the angle of the blade such that the bottom of the cut is shorter than the line drawn on the top of the board.

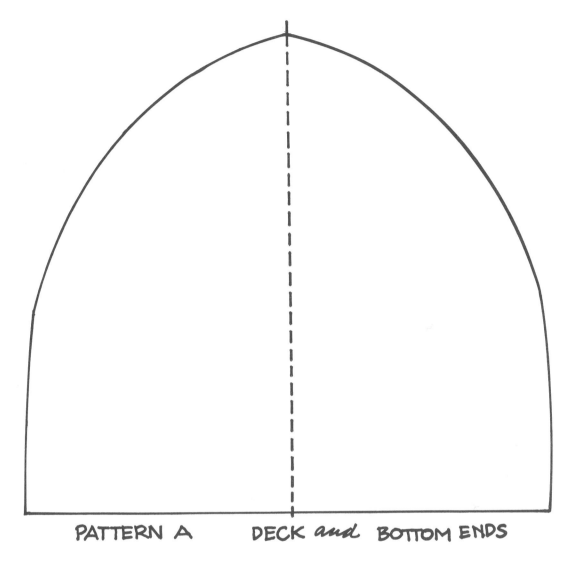

PATTERN A   DECK *and* BOTTOM ENDS

2. *Spacers* Draw an end-to-end centerline on the 9″ length of 2″x 6″ board. Using pattern A aligned on this centerline about 1″ from one end, trace the pattern. From the point of this tracing, measure along the centerline and mark at a distance of 7″. Reverse the pattern, place the point on this mark, and trace again. Cut on these lines so that the side with the lines has the SMALLER dimensions. To accomplish this, simply

make the cut in the opposite direction as you did for the first (bottom) piece. Now, cut this piece in half using a ninety-degree cut to make two spacers. Apply glue to each of the smaller sides of the 2"x 6" spacers and place one at each end of the bottom piece (Fig. 1). Spread the glue by twisting the pieces before aligning them to ensure a good bond. When aligned, set aside to dry.

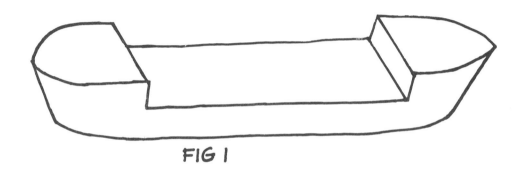

FIG 1

3. *Cabin* Cut two 12" pieces of 3⅝" width lattice. These will be the cabin side pieces. Draw a centerline on a 12" length of 1"x 4" pine, from end to end. Center pattern piece B on the board and cut two cabin end pieces. Glue and nail the cabin sides to the cabin ends using eight ¾" brads (centerlines to the outside). Position the top of the side ¼" below the start of the roof slope.

4. *Roof* From a piece of 5¼" lattice, cut two pieces: one 3⅞"x 13" and the other 1⅜"x 13". Set the smaller piece aside (this will be used in Step 7 for the bow and stern pieces). Cut one piece of 3⅝" lattice

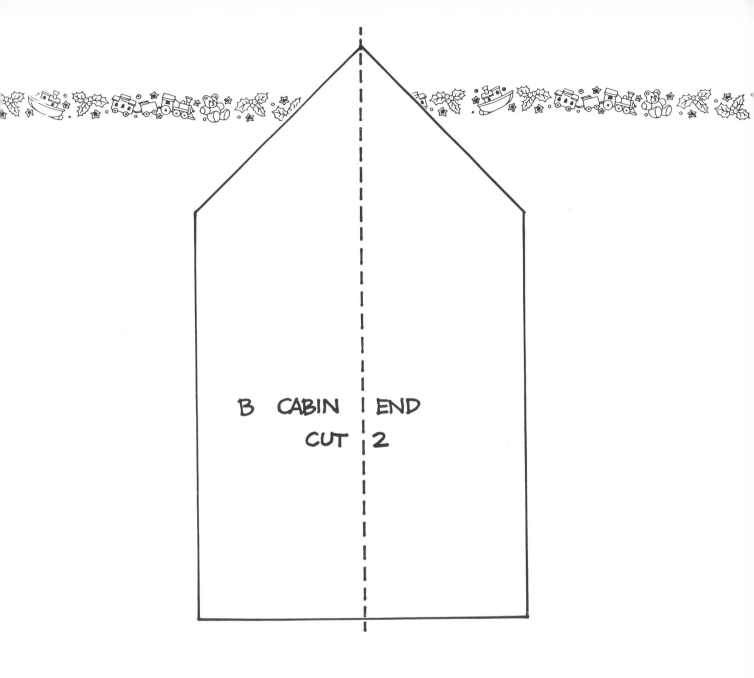

B CABIN END
CUT 2

to a length of 13". This is the other cabin roof piece. Using eight ¾"
brads and glue, center and nail both roof pieces to the end pieces: the
3⅝" piece flush with the peak of the end pieces; the 3⅞" piece
overlapping the smaller roof piece. Apply glue to this overlapped edge of
the smaller roof piece. Recess nails and cover with wood putty. Using a
⅛" drill bit, drill a hole at one end of the roof peak for positioning
the dove.

5. *Deck* Cut a piece of 1″ x 6″ to a length of approximately 24″. Draw an end-to-end centerline on this piece. Turn the deck piece over and place the hull assembly upside down on it. Align and trace both ends of the hull assembly onto the deck. Number each end of both the hull assembly and the deck so they can be assembled the same way. Cut the deck so that the top (the side with the centerline) has the LARGER dimensions. Center the cabin on the deck, matching centerline on deck with that drawn on the end pieces. Draw lines on the deck along the edge of the cabin END pieces only. Remove cabin and use a straight edge to connect the lines from end to end. Cut out this rectangular section of the deck using a saber saw set at ninety degrees. Round the edges of the cabin end pieces that fit into the deck, and, with the cabin in the same position as was used to draw the lines, check for fit. Sand deck or cabin end pieces if necessary. Remove cabin and set aside. Now apply glue to the top of the hull assembly and place the deck on it. Align and set aside.

6. *Bow/Stern* For the bow and stern pieces, trace pattern C on the 1⅜″ x 13″ piece of lattice set aside in Step 4. Cut, sand, and set aside.

7. *Hull Sides* Use pattern piece D to make the sides of the ark. Place top edge of the pattern on a factory edge of the ½″ plywood, grain parallel to the mark on the pattern. Trace all lines except for the

BOW/STERN

C

CUT 2

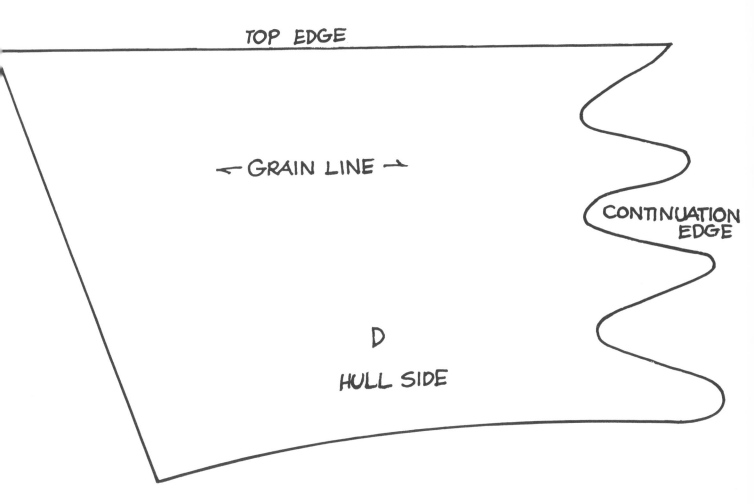

TOP EDGE

← GRAIN LINE →

CONTINUATION
EDGE

D

HULL SIDE

continuation end. Measure 25½″ from the point of the tracing along the top edge and mark. Turn the pattern over and, with the point on the mark, trace again in the same manner. Connect the ends of the drawn lines with a straight edge. Cut the piece using a fine saw blade. Use this piece to trace the second side piece. In order to facilitate easy turning when attaching these pieces to the bottom of the ark, the wood must be scored at each end (Fig. 2). Begin by placing the side piece on a work

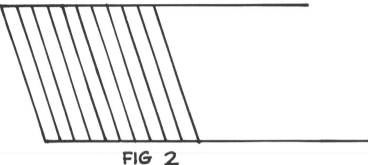

FIG 2

surface. Using a metal straight edge and a sharp utility knife, score a cut through the back-side layer of wood ¼″ from the end. Use three passes with light pressure rather than one pass with heavy pressure for better depth control. Now place another cut approximately ³⁄₃₂″ from the first cut in the same way. Continue this process of making parallel cuts in the end of the piece at ¼″ intervals until there are fifteen ''channels.'' Using the utility knife like a pencil, scrape (NOT CUT) a u-shaped channel from edge to edge to a depth slightly greater than one-half the plywood thickness. Repeat this process on the other end and on both ends of the other piece. Check to see if the channels are deep enough by gently bending the end to the approximate contour of the hull. Cuts too deep will reveal a crease on the finished side.

8. *Ark Sides* Using a Shurform™ plane, smooth the hull as shown in Fig. 3. Next, apply glue and center the bow/stern pieces at each end of the hull (use the top and bottom centerline marks) and nail, using four

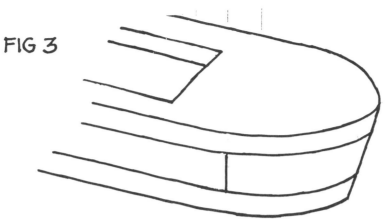

FIG 3

¾" brads. With the hull on its side, gently bend one side piece over the ends to check for fit. Use pressure to make the piece conform to the contour of the hull. If too long, trim with a knife or saw. When sized and centered, nail in place, from the center outward one end at a time, using 1" paneling nails. Repeat for other side piece, making sure both ends are positioned the same height above the deck. The important aspect of attaching the sides is that they fit at the bow and stern; overlap on the bottom is not a problem. To level the ark, trim the excess plywood from the bottom with a utility knife.

9. *Ramp* Use a utility knife to make a ⅛" wide channel ⅜" from one end of the ramp using the same technique as for the hull side pieces. Cut to a depth of ⅛". This will keep the ramp from sliding off the rim of the ark.

10. *Finishing* Paint the deck, ramp, and cabin sides tan. Paint the hull and roof rust. Paint shingle design on the roof. Transfer patterns to cabin

A

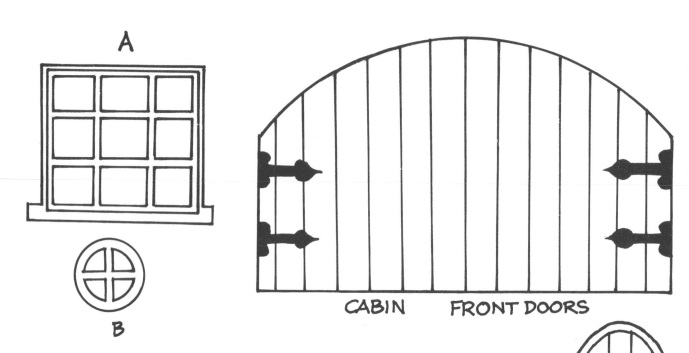

B

CABIN   FRONT DOORS

SIDE DOOR

as follow: three A windows on cabin back, a door and one B window at one end, one B window and one A window on the other end, two A windows and a large door on cabin front. Paint windows gray, outline windows, and paint mullions white. Add rust sills. Paint doors rust with black hardware. Optional: Antique by rubbing the ark with a mixture of turpentine and burnt umber oil paint.

FIGURES

Transfer patterns to ½″ pine (snakes are cut from ¼″ pine). Cut with a band or scroll saw. Sand edges and paint. Drill ⅛″ hole through Noah's hand, apply glue, and insert a twig staff. Drill ⅛″ hole into one dove, apply glue, and insert a 1½″ length of ⅛″ dowel. For tails, drill

DRILL

X MARKS TAIL PLACEMENT

a small hole and glue in yarn or thin strands of sisal twine. For a worn

appearance, sand lightly with fine grit sandpaper or antique by rubbing

each piece with a mixture of burnt umber oil and turpentine.

Scented Kindling Cones

A basket full of these scented fire starters will warm the heart as well as the home of your friends and what a wonderful way to use all those extra pinecones. If you don't happen to have any cones, the best time to collect them is in the early fall. Dry them in the sun until they open fully before using them for this project. The pleasant aroma of these cones can be enjoyed before burning, but when you are ready for a fire, simply tuck a few under your kindling and light. For a finishing touch, pile the cones into a decorated basket, embellish with sprigs of evergreen or dried flowers, and add a sprinkling of pinecone flowers.

SUPPLIES

two or three dozen medium to large pinecones

1½ lb. paraffin (broken into chunks)

scented oil

three or four crayons for tinting

double boiler or coffee can and pot

Supplies continued on the following page

newspaper

tongs

large basket

fabric for bow (18″ x 24″)

fabric stiffener

hot glue gun

clear acrylic spray or varnish

1. CAUTION! Hot wax is combustible, so never melt it over an open flame or direct heat. Insulate the wax by melting it in a double boiler or a coffee can (placed on a wire rack) inside a pot of hot water. Do not overheat the wax; once it is melted, turn the heat to low. To the wax, add two teaspoons of scented oil and the broken crayons. Using tongs, dip each pinecone into the wax; place on a newspaper until the wax hardens. Dip again until each cone is well coated.

2. For the bow, cut two pieces of fabric, each 23″ long by 7″ wide, and another piece 4″ long by 3″ wide. Place fabric stiffener in a flat-bottomed bowl and thoroughly coat both sides of each piece. Run the

fabric through your fingers, squeezing out excess stiffener. Overlap the long edges of each piece in the center, finger press creases, and hang until nearly dry (about 45 minutes). Notch both ends of one 23″ strip, wrap it around the basket handle, and glue in place. Overlap the short edges of the other 23″ strip to form a loop (keeping the overlapped area in the center), gather the center to form a bow; wrap the small strip of fabric around the center and glue on the back. Glue the bow to the basket and finish by spraying with a light coat of acrylic sealer or varnish.

3. To make pinecone flowers, hold a cone firmly in one hand and, using a pair of sharp wire cutters or pruning shears, cut through the middle of the cone about three rows up from the bottom. If cones are thick, you may have to twist and cut from both sides. From a 6″ cone you should get at least three flowers.

Orange Pomanders

Freshly cut evergreens, plump gingerbread people hot from the oven, and the sweet, enticing aroma of oranges (or lemons, limes, or apples) and spice are the scents of Christmas, equally as important as the sights and sounds. Here are some simple projects guaranteed to trigger some memories as they fill your home with the old-fashioned fragrances you remember from your childhood.

The age-old tradition of making pomander balls at Christmastime is a favorite one in many American homes. Plan on making lots of them; the spicy aroma of these clove-studded fruits will add such a festive touch to your holiday decorating.

SUPPLIES (TO MAKE FOUR)

four medium-sized oranges (or lemons, limes, apples)

eight tablespoons of cinnamon

one tablespoon of allspice

Supplies continued on the following page

one tablespoon of nutmeg

two tablespoons of powdered orrisroot

six ounces of whole cloves

1. Blend cinnamon, allspice, nutmeg, and orrisroot together to make the curing mixture.

2. With a nail, pierce the fruit and insert a clove. Cover the entire fruit, inserting cloves about ⅛″ apart. Roll the clove-studded fruit in the curing mixture.

3. Line a shoe box with tissue paper and place the pomanders in the box. Sprinkle with the remaining spice mixture. Cover the box and place in a warm, dry closet for about two to four weeks. When dried thoroughly, the pomanders will feel lighter and firm to the touch. Shake off excess powder and decorate with ribbon if desired.

Molded Beeswax Ornaments

These ornaments are so easy to make and will be enjoyed long after the cookies made from the molds are gone. If you don't have stoneware cookie molds, you can substitute plastic candy molds. Plastic molds need not be oiled. Although the natural honey scent and color is very appealing, for variety try tinting the melted beeswax with crayon pieces and/or scenting it with your favorite essential oil (one teaspoon per cup of melted wax). You can also highlight a part of the design with acrylic paint.

SUPPLIES

beeswax

stoneware cookie molds (or plastic)

spray vegetable oil

colored wax chips or crayons (optional)

scented oil (optional)

acrylic paints (optional)

ice pick

thin ribbon

1. Lightly spray stoneware cookie molds with oil.

2. CAUTION! Hot wax is combustible. Melt beeswax in the top of a double boiler or inside a coffee can placed in a pot of hot water. Add color chips and scented oil, if desired. Pour beeswax into molds and place on a level, newspaper-covered surface to harden. Edges will pull away from the mold. Remove the ornament by turning the mold over and gently tapping until the ornament falls into your hand. Pierce with a heated ice pick and thread ribbon through the hole for hanging. When using on a tree, be careful not to hang them near a light. Store in a cool place.

Reindeer

These whimsical reindeer with movable heads are so easy to make, don't stop until you have a whole herd of them prancing across your mantel or tree.

SUPPLIES

bundle of sticks and branches

4d finishing nails (one each)

cotton swabs

brown acrylic paint

wood glue

ribbon

small jingle bells

1. From a live branch (with an approximate diameter of 1″), cut a 3″ length for the body. For legs, from a branch with an approximate ¼″ diameter, cut four lengths, each about 3½″ long. Cut a 1¼″ length of

½″ branch for the neck. Cut a 1 to 1¼″ length of tapered ⅝″ branch as a head. For antlers choose two very thin twigs with many divisions.

2. Using a ⅛″ bit, drill four leg holes (sloped slightly outward—ten to fifteen degrees) on the underside of the body piece, spacing each about ¼″ from the end and about ⅜″ apart. For a tail, drill one hole on the body about ⅛″ from the end (perpendicular to the back). On the body top, drill one neck pilot hole, spacing it about ⁵⁄₁₆″ from the front end and sloping it to the front at about twenty degrees. At the top of the head, ¼″ from the end, drill a ⅛″ centered hole through the piece. Next to this hole (⅛″ away) drill an angled ⅛″ hole to a depth of about ¼″ for the antlers. Repeat on the other side of the head. Now use a ¼″ bit to redrill the leg holes, and a ⅜″ bit to redrill the neck hole.

3. Insert the neck into the hole in the body. The fit should be tight. If necessary, trim the bark to make it fit, glue, and drive it in with a hammer. Drive a 4d finishing nail into the center of the top end of the neck, leaving ½″ out to hold the head. Fit the head on the nail protruding from the neck. For a tight fit in the leg holes, trim the bark off the ends where necessary. When all four legs have been fitted, glue,

then rotate each so all "hooves" rest on a flat surface. Insert the antlers into the head. For a tail, cut the end from a cotton swab (leaving about ¼" of the stick attached), glue in place. Paint the tail brown. Decorate with ribbon and tiny jingle bells, if desired. To hang, attach a small eye hook to the center back, and thread with ribbon.

Wreath and Garland

Herald the season by fashioning this fragrant evergreen wreath and garland. Almost any type of evergreen will do, but if you will be using these decorations indoors, avoid spruce or hemlock, since they tend to drop their needles sooner.

SUPPLIES

Wreath:

Note: finished size 22 to 24 inches

16″ to 18″ three-ring wire wreath frame

spool of 28-gauge florist's wire

36 to 45 full sprigs of evergreen each about 12″ long

3½ yards of 2½″ wide ribbon

dried white German statice, sprigs of holly, small pinecones

glue gun

1. Attach a wire loop to the frame for hanging. Cut florist's wire into 12″ lengths (about 24).

2. Group three (or more if the sprigs are sparse) evergreen sprigs together and wrap a 12″ length of wire tightly around the ends. Continue until all sprigs have been wired. Depending on the fullness of the sprigs, twelve to fourteen bunches should be enough to cover the frame.

3. Wire evergreen bunches securely to the frame (all going in the same direction), overlapping one over the other until covered. Step back occasionally to check wreath for symmetry. Trim greens, and wire in extra sprigs where necessary. Wire holly and statice to the wreath. Glue small pinecones to statice. Finish with a fluffy bow.

SUPPLIES

Garland:

spool of 28-gauge florist's wire

10″ to 12″ long sprigs of evergreen (amount determined by desired length of garland)

1. Overlap sprigs of evergreen and wrap them together tightly with wire. Do not cut wire; use one continuous piece unwrapping from the spool as needed. If desired, decorate completed garland with bows, pinecones, or berries.

Bird's Nest Ornaments

Legend has it that the birds sang all night when Christ was born, so what could be a more appropriate and natural decoration than a flock of birds nesting in your Christmas tree? For a festive touch, tuck one into a favorite houseplant or on a grapevine or evergreen wreath.

SUPPLIES

cardboard

sheet moss

assorted dried materials (statice, baby's breath, yarrow,

    pinecones, artemesia)

small artificial bird

florist's wire

glue gun

1. Trace circle pattern to cardboard and cut. Poke two holes in the center of the cardboard, about ¾" apart. Insert a 12" length of wire

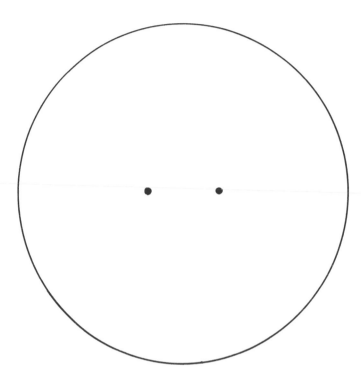

through holes (equal amount extending through each hole) and twist together tightly on the reverse side of the cardboad. These wire extensions will be used to attach the ornament to the tree branch. Fold wire flat while working on the ornament.

2. Glue sheet moss to cover one side and edges of the cardboard circle. Make a small indentation in the center and glue bird in place.

3. Next, attach dried flowers, weeds, or pinecones to the base with glue. Finish with a small bow.

CAROLS

The Christmas Carol Tradition

It has probably happened to you. It's two days before Christmas. Everyone has just been out shopping and last-minute purchases, still in their bags, are stashed in various corners of the house. The kids are impatiently waiting for their soup to be served so they can wrap their presents before going to bed. The atmosphere is charged with a pleasant mix of exhaustion and exhilaration. And the weatherman was right: It's starting to snow.

Then, over the chatter of the kids' excited conversation, you hear singing. Somebody has come to serenade you. The whole family runs toward the familiar sound. The kids take an embarrassed peek out the window, but you go right to the front door and open it.

"Hark! the her-ald an-gels si-ng, 'Glory to the new-born King'." Standing in a semicircle on the front lawn are a dozen people, most of whom you don't even know. They're singing to you. Wearing thick mittens and gloves, they're busy balancing their candles and those ubiquitous little songbooks distributed free by one of the major life insurance companies. Some are wearing ski caps; others are bareheaded. There are all ages of adults, teenagers, and children, and they all appear to be part of the choir at the church down the street just out for a night of singing. They're caroling.

The caroling tradition as we know it today started in the nineteenth century in England. But "caroling," by its strict definition of singing and circle dancing, goes back much further than nineteenth-century England. Some historians date caroling back to around 5000 B.C. to Eridu, an ancient city located between the Tigris and Euphrates rivers in Mesopotamia. Shortly after the harvest season, young men, adorned in celebration dress, traditionally danced a circle dance to lyre, pipe, and drum music. They would begin by standing in a circle to symbolize the never-ending cycle of life. While people around them chanted and played, they executed a series of steps that gradually took the circle closer to the temple. There, gifts were made to the gods in thanks for the bountiful season and another year of life. When the ceremonies ended, a grand feast was held. This ritual: worship, gift-giving, chanting, feasting, had all the ingredients of our latter-day Christian celebration. Later the Romans perfected the end-of-the-year ritual. Each winter solstice, the Romans set aside several days for "Saturnalia." Saturn was the god of agriculture. During Saturnalia slaves were served by their masters. Gifts of wax candles, preserved sweetmeats, writing tablets, napkins, and paste-like images of fruit and dolls were exchanged. The Romans also bedecked their homes with evergreens, denoting everlasting life, and decorated the greens with bits of colored paper, fruits, and the paste images.

These Roman pagan traditions, however, clashed with the newly-established Christian church. The church held that honoring the birthday of Christ should be treated with solemnity. Church authorities could not reconcile their customs with those of people who danced, sang, and feasted. This disagreement lasted several hundred years until St. Francis of Assisi thought of a way for reconciliation.

In 1223, St. Francis, with the consent of the Pope, conducted a Christmas midnight Mass using dance, songs, and a manger scene complete with live animals. In a short time, Christmas celebrations, as we now know them, began to take shape all over the world.

For the next three centuries this marriage seemed to be a happy one. Caroling was not only acceptable but widely practiced. The English added words which meant that carols were not only intended to be danced but sung.

In those pre-Columbus days of Christmas songwriting, authors knew little of the world and they would incorporate verse that assumed Bethelehem was like their own country. Consequently, carols from the northlands told of ice and snow; those from southern climes included references to flowers and birds; and from England came carols that dealt with the sea (doesn't everyone live on a coast?). "I Saw Three Ships" contains words that have ships sailing into Bethlehem's alleged harbor, for example.

Also, since music writing was a relatively new art form and practiced by a limited number of composers, carols were often developed by word of mouth. People would make up verses on the spot and sing them to tunes that had been handed down over the years. Such carols as "The First Nowell," which has no written history, may have been created that way. Many carols we enjoy today were created first as poems or hymns, originally sung to standard tunes known by generic titles, and eventually "married" to a particular tune that was most favorably accepted by the public. A good case in point would be "Hark! the Herald Angels Sing," a carol that was first a hymn (the poem only) created by Charles Wesley in 1739, no doubt sung to one tune or another for over a hundred years, before being matched to a tune composed by Felix Mendelssohn for an entirely different occasion.

But we're getting ahead of ourselves. Back to England, clearly a country that exercised great influence over today's Christmas customs. During the seventeenth century, the country underwent great political and religious conflict. In 1647, Cromwell's parliament literally banned Christmas celebrations of any type. Although the decree was only in effect for twelve years, its influence was widely felt.

Even though the pilgrims who settled New England were themselves in conflict with the Anglican church and moved to the New World to pursue "religious freedom," they imposed a prohibition on Christmas celebrations. The Puritans, Baptists, Quakers, and Presbyterians all considered Christmas Day an "abomination." Since the Bible gave no reference to such an observance, they felt it was neither the Pope's nor any government's place to sanction an official celebration. In one much-quoted story from 1621, Governor Bradford of the Massachusetts colony sharply rebuked some young men who stayed home to play games on Christmas while others went off to work. In 1659, the General Court of Massachusetts declared that "whosoever shall be found observing any such days as Christmas or the like, either by forebearance of labor or feasting, or in any other way as a festival, shall be fined five shillings."

Still, Christmas did have a minor foothold in the New World. The first New England celebration was held in 1604 on an island off the coast of northern Maine. Explorer John Smith sailed out of Jamestown in 1614 and into a bay on the midcoast of Maine on Christmas Day. He called the bay Christmas Cove, the name it bears today.

Although the 1659 Massachusetts Bay law was repealed twenty-six years later, habits had become set and New England was to be nearly Christmas-less until the middle of the nineteenth century. Colleges didn't observe the holiday until after 1847. In Boston, Christmas was a regular workday through 1856 and there were classes in public schools on that day until 1870. In fact, the entire concept of Christmas was virtually dying out in the early part of the nineteenth century until a particular book crossed the Atlantic and began to turn the public mind back to thoughts of what Christmas really meant.

In 1843 Charles Dickens, already a popular figure on both sides of the Atlantic, published his *A Christmas Carol*. The sentiment expressed in the moving story put Christmas back on the calendar. His tour of the United States a few years later, hosted by the popular American author Washington Irving, put great emphasis on *A Christmas Carol* and from that point on, it was a rapid upward climb for the reinstatement of Christmas into public life.

The first New England state to legalize Christmas as a holiday was Connecticut in 1845. The other states soon followed: Vermont, 1850; New Hampshire, 1851; Rhode Island, 1852; Massachusetts, 1855; and Maine, 1858.

The religious conflict that created the Christmas prohibition was eventually put to rest as more and more immigrants penetrated the shores of New England. Swedes, Germans, Poles, and Italians, already much accustomed to celebrating Christmas with songs, gifts, and feasts cast a great influence over the conservative New Englanders. Christmas trees in homes began to make their regular appearance as early as the 1830s, although Hessian soldiers are thought to have introduced the Christmas tree to America during the Revolutionary War. The first White House tree was installed by Franklin Pierce, a Bowdoin College graduate.

Finally, after several millennia of merged customs, mixed languages, and the mutual agreement of church and state, Christmas – the day, the event, the tradition – took on a recognizable life of its own. One of the happiest and most-widely-practiced customs of Christmas still today is the singing of carols.

The complete history of carols could take up volumes. Thousands of them have been written over the centuries, but most have been lost. Those that remain popular come from so many sources that few generalities can be applied as to their origin. Certainly pagan customs abound as evidenced in the words in "Deck the Halls," and legend provides the source material as in "Good King Wenceslas."

While carols have originated in a number of different countries, it appears that many of the popular ones had their beginnings in England. "God Rest Ye Merry, Gentlemen" originated in the streets of London as sung by "waits" (paid performers). "Here We Come A'Wassailing" is derived from the custom the English developed of calling on friends and strangers alike during the holidays for a drink from the ever-present wassail bowl. "Wassail" comes from the twelfth-century Saxon toast "wase hael," meaning "be in health," as servants paid tribute to their masters.

If indeed one generality can be stated, it is that most carols appear to have developed from poems. While many publications of popular and classical music credit the composers, Christmas carols by and large owe their beginnings to the authors. The words usually inspired the music, or inspired someone to set those words to someone else's tunes, those tunes frequently having been written with no thought of Christmas. It was the passage of time that kindled many a carol's popularity and blended or obscured the original reasons for its creation.

What follows is music for and a history of twelve Christmas carols traditionally sung in New England. Each carol was born of inspiration nurtured by time and preserved for the generations ahead by those who believe in keeping and celebrating the singing tradition of Christmas.

The arrangements for these carols have been provided by Michael Braz, who is currently Assistant Professor of Music at Georgia Southern University. He has arranged music for symphony orchestra, concert band, folk singers, jazz ensembles, and choruses. The music was prepared for publication on a computer by Terry White of Westbrook, Maine. I express my sincere thanks and appreciation to both these gentlemen for their time and talents.

Russell I. Burleigh

Joy to the World

There are many fascinating aspects to this very joyous and popular Christmas carol. One of the most fascinating is the author himself.

Isaac Watts overcame many difficulties to become one of the most prolific of hymn writers and a strong and influential leader in bringing about changes in the Church. He was born in Southhampton, England, in 1674, the son of a nonconformist who was jailed repeatedly for defying authorities.

Isaac was skinny and frail, with a hooked nose and a head too large for his body. He learned Latin at four, Greek at nine, French and Hebrew by the time he was thirteen. At fifteen he was writing hymns for his church's congregation.

Friends of Watts offered to pay his way to Oxford but he declined, opting instead to study privately. At twenty-six he was made pastor of a church in London and held no other position for the rest of his life. When his health failed in 1708, he offered to resign but the congregation insisted he stay and hired an assistant to help him.

One of his wealthy parishioners invited the sickly minister to his estate to rest. The intended weekend visit turned into a thirty-six-year stay, until his death in 1748. There, in the midst of quiet country life, he did most of his writing, which consisted of fifty-two books and several hundred hymns. He wrote "Joy to the World" in 1719.

Watts was the originator of the hymn writing which, as he put it, "imitated" the psalms, in effect, making the early writing conform to contemporary times. "Joy to the World" is an imitation, or paraphrase, of Psalm 98: "Make a joyful noise unto the Lord all the earth." The carol was published in 1719 in a collection called The Psalms of David in the Language of the New Testament. The music has sometimes been attributed to Handel, but only because of similarities to sections of the Messiah. Actually, the music was arranged and probably composed by American composer and educator Lowell Mason in 1839.

Joy to the World

Isaac Watts (1674-1748)

Lowell Mason (1792-1872)
arr. Michael Braz

Silent Night

The world's most universally popular Christmas carol was written in a matter of hours in a somewhat desperate situation, and its authors never knew what it was they had created.

In the little town of Oberndorf, near Salzburg, Austria, was a small church whose assistant pastor was twenty-five-year-old Joseph Mohr. As Christmas approached in 1818, organist Franz Gruber informed Mohr that mice had damaged the organ. It could not be played and the repairman was not due until after Christmas.

Pastor Mohr was beside himself because he especially wanted this service to go well in his young ministry. He played the guitar, but the music the choir had been rehearsing was too complex for that. If only there were some simpler music.

Then he thought of the night before when he had been so inspired by a Christmas play that afterward he had climbed a hill overlooking the village and the night had been so peaceful. Suddenly the words came to him: "Stille nacht! Heilige nacht!" He quickly finished the poem and prevailed on Franz Gruber to compose a tune for it.

With no time for proper rehearsal with the choir, "Silent Night" had its world premiere on Christmas morning with Franz Gruber strumming his guitar, singing the verses with Mohr, and the choir joining in on the final two lines.

Days later when Karl Mauracher, the organ repairman, arrived Mohr and Gruber proudly sang their new composition for him. Throughout his travels repairing organs, Mauracher told others of "Silent Night," the song born of necessity. Days stretched into years. The song was passed from person to person and gained in popularity. The Strasser Sisters, a group famed for its singing of Tyrolian mountain songs, added it to their repertory and "Silent Night" was heard in many countries throughout Europe. Joseph Mohr and Franz Gruber were forgotten.

The first published version appeared in 1833, another in 1840. Changes in both text and song had crept in, and the original authors remained uncredited. In 1854, the King of Prussia, Frederick William IV, heard a stirring performance by a large choir and declared that from that time on "Silent Night" should be included in *all Christmas performances in his country. Court musicians in Berlin were sent out to uncover its origin. Thinking that it might have been composed by Michael Haydn, son of noted composer Franz Josef, they inquired of St. Peter's Church in Salzburg as to the original manuscript.*

By chance, Franz Gruber's youngest son, a choirboy at St. Peter's, learned of the inquiry and obtained from his father a written account of the song's creation. But Joseph Mohr had died in 1848, at the age of fifty-five. He probably never knew that his trek up a hill overlooking Oberndorf had inspired the world's most beloved Christmas carol.

Franz Gruber was an organist at Hellein at the time of his death in 1863. Although the little church of St. Nicholas was washed away in a flood and a new one built in its place, Franz Gruber's guitar, the instrument that temporarily replaced the broken organ, was carefully preserved.

Silent Night

Joseph Mohr (1792-1848)

Franz Gruber (1787-1863)
arr. Michael Braz

We Three Kings of Orient Are

"We Three Kings of Orient Are" is a carol that enjoys several distinctions, but most distinctive of all was the man who wrote it. During his lifetime, John Henry Hopkins wrote church music, founded the respected Church Journal, designed church vestments and furniture, and created stained glass windows. He also served as rector of Christ Church, Williamsport, Pennsylvania, where he generously ministered to the poor and elderly.

Hopkins was born in Pittsburgh, Pennsylvania, in 1820, the son of an Episcopal minister. He grew up in Vermont where his father served as Bishop. After graduating with honors from the University of Vermont in 1839, Hopkins worked as a reporter in New York. Later influenced by a church conference he attended in London with his father, he enrolled in the General Theological Seminary in New York. After graduation in 1850, he stayed on to teach music.

While teaching at the seminary, Hopkins wrote a complete Christmas pageant, from script to music. Included in this impressive venture was a carol about the visit of the three Wise Men to the manger in Bethlehem.

Hopkins' carol is known worldwide. For a long time, however, *the carol was not thought of as American in origin. Because of the unusual folk-like nature of the minor mode music, publishers listed Hopkins as the arranger, thinking the carol was from sixteenth- or seventeenth-century Europe.*

"We Three Kings" enjoys other distinctions as well. It's one of the few carols still in common use that was written in America, one of few whose words and music were written by the same person, one of a very few written in a minor key, and almost the only one that relates the story of the Wise Men.

Originally published in an early collection of Hopkins' works, the carol became more widely known through his book of 1883, Poems by the Wayside Written During More Than Forty Years. It has since been translated into more than fourteen languages and included as a rare American carol in the Oxford Book of Carols. The British postal service even used it in a set of five Christmas Carol Stamps issued in 1982.

"We Three Kings" is the product of a man who was known variously as a scholar, writer, preacher, musician, poet, and artist, and above all, as a remarkable humanitarian.

We Three Kings of Orient Are

John Henry Hopkins Jr. (1820-1891)

John Henry Hopkins, Jr.
arr. Michael Braz

won - der, star of night, Star with roy - al

beau - ty bright, West - ward lead - ing still pro -

ceed - ing Guide us to Thy per - fect light.

Deck the Halls

While undoubtedly a "must" song for caroling, "Deck the Halls" probably has the most dubious history. The music is most commonly thought to be of Welsh origin. The words might actually be American, and one source credits Washington Irving. Regardless of the carol's history, the fact is that the words, more than any other carol, give us a nearly complete poetic description of today's Christmas celebrations.

We "deck the halls" with holly. The use of holly dates to pre-Christian times when, along with other plants that remained green during the winter, holly came to symbolize everlasting life. Then it was taken up by Christians who believed the cross on which Christ died was holly wood. With its prickly leaves, it was also a reminder of Christ's crown of thorns, the red berries symbolizing blood.

These days we "don our gay apparel" in the form of all sorts of bright red and green clothing. But holiday periods have always meant dress-up time for all civilizations.

The "blazing yule" log is again a throwback to pagan times. The word "yule" comes from a Scandinavian word for wheel which denoted the cycle of a year. Servants were sent into the forest to find the largest water-soaked log possible, for the celebration of the winter solstice lasted as many days as the yule log burned!

To "strike the harp and join the chorus" refers, of course, to carol singing. And finally, "fast away the old year passes" puts us in mind of when celebrations at this time of year first began.

Deck the Halls

Traditional

Old Welsh Air
arr. Michael Braz

The First Nowell

"The First Nowell" is a carol that developed spontaneously. In the seventeenth century, it was commonplace for folks to make up tunes and words on the spot. Somebody must have begun telling the story of Christmas one night – in words and song – and the song struck a responsive chord with everyone listening. Repetition of the song established its place in popular carol literature.

If this was the manner in which "The First Nowell" was created, it explains why the words don't exactly fit the music – many words are stretched over a number of notes at a time – and why the text contains inaccuracies. The carol has the shepherds, not the Wise Men, sighting the star "shining in the east." In a later verse, the star draws "nigh to the northwest."

The music may be French or English in origin. Both words and music were finally published in their present form in 1833 by William Sandys in his collection, Christmas Carols, Ancient and Modern.

The word "nowell" is an anglicized version of the French "noël." Some references claim the word has evolved from the Latin for birth, "natalis." Others hold that "novella," Latin for "news" is a more likely source word. Certainly the spelling is more closely related and the meaning is just as appropriate.

The carol is popular because of its story and melody line and because of its chorus, which can be sung quite dramatically. But part of its intrigue is its mystery, not unlike that of so many legends that have grown up around Christmas.

The First Nowell

Traditional

French - English
arr. Michael Braz

The first Now - ell the an - gel did say Was to cer - tain poor
They look - ed up and saw a Star Shin ing in the
This star drew nigh to the north - west, O'er Beth - le -
Then en - tered in those wise men three, Full rev - 'rent -

shepherds in fields as they lay; In fields where they lay keep-ing their
East, be - yond them far, And to the earth it both
hem it took its rest, And there it did it gave great
ly up - on their knee, And of - fered there, both in His pres -

sheep On a cold win-ter's night that was so deep. Now - ell, Now -
light, And so it con - tin - ued both day and night.
stay Right o - ver the place where Je - sus lay.
ence, Their gold and myrrh and frank - in - cense

ell, Now - ell, Now - ell, Born is the King of Is - ra - el.

Hark! the Herald Angels Sing

It's not unusual for the words of a carol to have been written by one person and the music composed by another – even years apart. "Hark! the Herald Angels Sing" is in this category. The carol, an amalgamation of work by four different gentlemen spanning 118 years, has resulted in one of the most beloved and rousing Christmas carols of all time.

Born the eighteenth child of a hardworking Anglican clergyman, Charles Wesley grew up in an England that was far different from his parents' teachings. The Anglican church was literally for sale in the first half of the eighteenth century. Important church positions paid handsomely and went to the most callously ambitious. The Anglican Church ignored the social ills of the day – gin mills thrived, children were sold for profit, and debtors' prisons overflowed.

Charles and his older brother John received an early classical education, then attended Christ Church, Oxford, expecting to be enmeshed in religious teachings. They were quickly disillusioned. After graduation, they both signed on to work in the new colony of Georgia, John as an Anglican chaplain and Charles as secretary to Governor Oglethorpe. They sailed in early 1736.

Sailing with them was a group of Moravians. The brothers were enchanted with members of this cheerful Christian sect who spent much of the voyage singing hymns, even during an intense storm that had all the other passengers huddled together with fright. Charles and John were impressed not only by the calmness of the Moravians in the face of danger but also by their hymn singing, something Anglicans did not do.

Once settled in Georgia, John immediately began writing hymns and setting them to music. He published a small collection and used the book in his chapel services. It was the first use of a hymnal in an Anglican church.

Being handsome men with engaging personalities, Charles and John tended to attract the ladies of the Georgia colony. This eventually caused Governor Oglethorpe, who prohibited his staff from consorting with women, to dismiss Charles.

The brothers returned to England together, and remembering their experience with the Moravians, decided to join Aldersgate, a Moravian mission. The serenity of the mission and the teaching of the brethren led both Charles and John to experience religious conversions. John gained more conviction to carry out his mission of preaching countrywide. Charles decided to devote his life to hymn writing and to work to upgrade the life of the poor and oppressed. It was the beginning of the Methodist movement.

Although Charles wrote 6,500 hymns over his lifetime, the best were created shortly after his conversion. In 1738, he created a poem he called "Hark! How all the welkin rings, Glory to the King of Kings," a hymn whose subject was the Incarnation. "Welkin" is an archaic word meaning "heaven."

It was a friend and publisher of Wesley's hymns, George Whitefield, who changed the lines to "Hark! the herald angels sing, Glory to the newborn King!" The change not only annoyed Wesley but recategorized the hymn to a Christmas theme.

Over a hundred years later, in 1840, Felix Mendelssohn composed a cantata on the occasion of the three hundredth anniversary of the invention of the printing press. Singling out a particular section of the work, he wrote: "I think there ought to be other words to [this tune] . . . but it will never do to be sacred words . . . something gay and popular, as the music tries to do."

Mendelssohn died in 1847 and nine years later Westminster Abbey organist William Cummings became the fourth man in the process of creating a famous carol. He joined Charles Wesley's words to Mendelssohn's cantata and "Hark! the Herald Angels Sing" as we know it today was first sung.

Hark! the Herald Angels Sing

Charles Wesley (1707-1788)

Felix Mendelssohn (1809-1847)

arr. Michael Braz

ood King Wenceslas

"Good King Wenceslas" has the most unusual and longest history of any carol sung today. It resulted from a poem written by a nineteenth-century Englishman. The poem is about a tenth-century Bohemian Duke who became legendary because he practiced the Christian teachings of a first-century martyr. And the poem was set to a sixteenth-century Scandinavian tune.

"Good King Wenceslas" was actually a Duke of Bohemia, now a part of Czechoslovakia. Popes hadn't yet begun to bestow the title of "King" on Christian rulers in the tenth century. As a devout Christian, he believed in and practiced the teachings of the martyred St. Stephen, whose feast is celebrated on December 26.

Stephen was a Jew who converted to Christianity. As an evangelist, he effectively converted other Jews. His principal concern was looking after poor widows and other unfortunates, and he criticized the Sanhedrin, the rabbinic ruling body of Jerusalem, for not extending the same care. In A.D. 38, Stephen's words of defense at a hearing so stirred up a mob that they stoned him to death, an act that led to his sainthood.

During cold winter months, Wenceslas would visit the countryside to see how his people were faring. Whenever he found someone in need of food or firewood, he ordered his servants to provide it from the castle stores.

But as much as Wenceslas's reputation and the love his people felt for him grew, so too did the bitter hatred and jealousy of his envious younger brother, Boleslav. Boleslav had his own followers who were dissatisfied with Wenceslas's settlement of a border dispute.

One day, in the year 935, Wenceslas prepared to attend church in Prague for a few moments of prayer. As he knelt at the altar he felt the presence of two figures on either side of him. Without warning, both men drove daggers into the body of the young Duke and left him to die at the altar. Boleslav was known to be responsible for the assassination, yet he assumed the throne and title of Duke of Bohemia, ruling the country for the next several years.

Although the legend of the beloved Duke stands out in the recorded history of Bohemia, the man might have remained known only to Bohemia were it not for a noted English hymnist. Dr. John Mason Neale (1818–1866), a clergyman responsible for several well-known translations and hymns we sing today, chose the subject of the Duke of Bohemia for a poem he wrote for children to emphasize selflessness and generosity at Christmastime. It was Neale who, in his 1853 poem, provided the Duke with a new title and anglicized his name. (The famous Wenceslas Square in Prague, with its prominent statue, is named after the martyred Duke.)

For the music, Neale turned to a very early publication, Piae

Cantiones (Sacred Songs), *a collection of Scandinavian tunes compiled by Martin Luther and published in 1582. "Good King Wenceslas" was set by Neale to an old spring carol "Tempus Adest Floridum" ("Spring Has Now Unwrapped Her Flowers") whose words have long been lost. Sir John Stainer, a friend of Neale, harmonized the music.*

Despite the relative popularity of "Good King Wenceslas" over the years, the authoritative Oxford Book of Carols nevertheless takes the carol, and particularly Neale, to task, calling it one of Neale's "less happy pieces" and quoting other authorities who term the poem "doggeral" and "poor and commonplace to the last degree." The book continues by suggesting "not without hope that, with the present wealth of carols for Christmas, 'Good King Wenceslas' may gradually pass into disuse, and the tune restored to spring-time." This is not likely to happen now that the carol has survived nearly into the twenty-first century — a carol whose inspiration dates from A.D. 38, only mere decades after the occurrence for which Christmas carols are sung.

Good King Wenceslas

John Mason Neale (1818-1866)

Music: "Tempus adest floridum" from Piae Cantiones (1582)
Words by John Mason Neale (1818–1866)

Little Town of Bethlehem

Phillips Brooks, born in Boston in 1835, was the son of parents who put great emphasis on his education and religious upbringing. After graduating from Harvard, he briefly taught at the Boston Latin School.

But it was teaching of a different nature that was to be Brooks' calling. He enrolled in the Episcopal Theological Seminary in Alexandria, Virginia, beginning a long and distinguished career in the ministry. Ordained in 1859, he became Rector of the small Church of the Advent in Philadelphia, moving over to Holy Trinity in January 1862.

Brooks had a popular following at Holy Trinity. Within a short time, the two, and even three, Sunday services were full to overflowing. Wednesday evening services in the chapel had to be moved to the church to accommodate the crowds.

Brooks gave his all to his calling. He helped Lewis Redner, Holy Trinity's church organist and Sunday School superintendent, build a large attendance. When Brooks perceived Philadelphia's apathy to the threat of a Confederate invasion, he organized a citywide march of ministers on the Mayor's office. After the battle at

Gettysburg, he joined a team of volunteers and headed for the battle-field to attend the wounded, Confederate and Union alike. Abhorring slavery, he demonstrated a special affinity for blacks, helping them gain access to Philadelphia's streetcars.

By 1865, he had gained so much love and respect from his parishioners that they rewarded him with a twelve-month leave that included full pay. He elected to use the time to visit the British Isles, continental Europe, and Palestine.

On Christmas Eve, only days before the end of his year-long journey, Brooks found himself in the hills overlooking Bethlehem. He had traveled on horseback to the place where shepherds had looked after their sheep since before the time the angels visited them. He returned to Bethlehem in time for a five-hour Christmas Eve service at the basilica built by Constantine over the original manger. Brooks later wrote the children of his Sunday School: "I remember especially on Christmas Eve when I was standing in the old church in Bethlehem, close to the spot where Jesus was born . . . it seemed as if I could hear voices . . . telling each other of the 'Wonderful Night' of the Saviour's birth."

It was three years later in Philadelphia that he drew on his memories of that eventful trip. Wishing to create something extra special for his Sunday School children for Christmas 1868, he drew on his memorable experience and wrote a poem: "O little town of Bethlehem, how still we see thee lie . . ."

He asked Lewis Redner to write a tune for the hymn so he could present it to the children on a particular Sunday. Redner had no tune ready on the Saturday night before and went to bed uninspired. During the night he was suddenly jolted awake with what he referred to later as "an angel strain" running through his head. Feverishly, he wrote down the melody, then filled in the harmony the next morning in time for Sunday School. Eventually published in 1892, the carol soon became a world favorite. Phillips Brooks became Bishop of Massachusetts in 1891 but died only two years later.

Phillips Brooks' love for children was evidenced by his deeds. But the love children felt for him was summed up by a little five-year-old girl who, upon learning of his death, exclaimed: "Oh, mama, how happy the angels will be."

O Little Town of Bethlehem

Phillips Brooks (1835-1893)

Lewis H. Redner (1831-1908)

arr. Michael Braz

Come, All Ye Faithful

For over two hundred years, this Christmas carol has gained such fame and popularity that it is now known in over 125 languages.

"Adeste fidelis, laeti triumphantes." The words themselves inspire us all to sing beyond our capacity each holiday season. Yet their true origin was unknown for two centuries.

It was thought, for example, that the Latin text came from an anonymous author in Germany, or perhaps France. And the well-known tune was attributed to Portugal. But in 1946, an English vicar, Dom John Stephan of Buckfast Abbey, happened across some original manuscripts created by John Francis Wade, born in England in 1712.

Douay, France, with its English Catholic college, was home to many politico-religious refugees from England during the mid-eighteenth century. Wade was one of them. He had moved to Douay in about 1740 and, as a Latin lay teacher in this Catholic community, made his living by copying and selling manuscripts of music.

After studying the manuscripts in his possession, Dom Stephan determined that the watermarks dated from Wade's time. In addition, Wade's manuscript of "Adeste Fidelis" included some incorrect Latin, possibly indicating his unfamiliarity with the Catholic liturgy. In 1750, a manuscript of Wade's "Cantus Diversi" containing the text and what is now thought to be his own tune of "Adeste Fidelis" was used in the English Roman Catholic College in Lisbon, Portugal. As the music was also used in the Portuguese embassy in London, the tune received the name "Portuguese hymn," further adding to the confusion.

Although forty English translations of the Latin text have been made, the one which is most commonly used, "O Come, All Ye Faithful," is by Latin scholar Frederick Oakeley. Oakeley was a London clergyman who wrote his translation in 1841. John Francis Wade died in 1786 at the age of seventy-five in Douay.

O Come, All Ye Faithful

Trans. Frederick Oakeley (1802-1880)

John Francis Wade (1712-1786)

arr. Michael Braz

ni - te ad - o - re - mus Do - num.
come let us a - dore Him,___ Christ,_____ the Lord.

rit.

It Came Upon the Midnight Clear

It probably isn't often that a successful venture results from the efforts of both a Harvard and a Yale man, but "It Came Upon the Midnight Clear" is a carol that came out of just such a combination.

Dr. Edmund Hamilton Sears was born in the Massachusetts Berkshires, educated at Union College and the Harvard Divinity School, and spent nearly all his ministry at a church in Wayland, Massachusetts. Sears was a fierce abolitionist and preached sermons and wrote papers condemning slavery. Much sought after as a speaker, he refused many offers because he was shy, not in good health, and had a frail speaking voice.

One cold December evening in 1849, he was sitting by the fire at the parsonage in Wayland when he began to write a poem. The poem was destined to become a classic American Christmas carol: "It came upon the midnight clear, that glorious song of old; from angels bending near the earth to touch their harps of gold."

Sears submitted the poem to the Christian Register in Boston *the following year, and it was published in the 1850 Christmas edition. Later the poem appeared in two British publications.*

Coincidentally, a young composer, Richard Storrs Willis, had written a song simply called "Study No. 23" in 1850, the same year as the poem's first publication. Willis, born in Boston to the son of the editor of the Youth's Companion, *was himself heavily involved in journalistic activities. He had also served on the faculty of Yale University, teaching German, and had spent time in Europe studying music with Felix Mendelssohn.*

The words and music from these two men were joined some years later by Uzziah C. Burnap, although the poem has been set to many other tunes as well.

Sears died in 1876 following a long illness. Willis died in Detroit, Michigan, in 1900. Sears and Willis though both New Englanders, probably never met. But they created a carol that is a favorite throughout the world.

It Came Upon the Midnight Clear

Edmund Hamilton Sears (1810-1876)

Richard Storrs Willis (1819-1900)

arr. Michael Braz

I Heard the Bells on Christmas Day

Henry Wadsworth Longfellow, America's foremost poet, wrote a poem that was born of despair and gloom. When set to music, it soon became a carol that epitomized the triumph of hope over hopelessness.

Longfellow was born in 1807 in Portland, Maine. When he was six months old, his parents moved into a brick home on Congress Street, the main thoroughfare of Portland. Today, that home serves as a museum and monument to the great poet.

At fourteen, Longfellow was enrolled in Bowdoin College in Brunswick. The class of 1825 later became known for its disproportionate share of notables: Longfellow, his lifelong friend and fellow author Nathaniel Hawthorne, and future U.S. president Franklin Pierce, among others. By 1860, Longfellow was an established figure throughout the world, having authored some of the most dramatic and memorable poetry ever created.

In 1861, tragedy struck Longfellow. His wife was killed in a fire. Only months later, the Civil War began and Longfellow was pushed deeper into a state of intense sadness. In December 1863, just after the battle of Gettysburg, Longfellow was residing at his home in Cambridge, Massachusetts. He had received word that his son, a lieutenant in the Army of the Potomac, had been seriously wounded in battle.

As he pondered all these events, he heard the pealing of church bells as they heralded Christmas Day. The sound continued for a long time. He took up his pen and wrote the bitter words "And in despair I bowed my head: 'there is no peace on earth,' I said, 'for hate is strong and mocks the song of peace on earth, good will to men.'"

But as he wrote, the bells began to lift his spirits and his poem reflected his thoughts: "Then pealed the bells more loud and deep. God is not dead nor doth he sleep! The wrong shall fail, the right prevail, with peace on earth, good will to men."

Although Longfellow never intended his words to be set to music, several composers and arrangers saw fit to do just that. The first coupling was with the tune "Illsley" by Henry Bishop (1665–1737). In modern times, noted popular songwriter Johnny Marks (of "Rudolph" fame) set the words to a beautiful melody. But the music most commonly used is by John Baptiste Calkin, a popular English organist and prolific composer, who wrote the music in 1872. Today, the carol is sung worldwide.

I Heard the Bells on Christmas Day

Henry Wadsworth Longfellow (1807-1882)

John Baptiste Calkin (1829-1905)

arr. Michael Braz

Holy Night

Born in 1803 in Paris, Adolphe Charles Adam seemed destined for a life of music since his father, Louis Adam, was a noted professor at the Paris Conservatory. But when Adolphe showed interest in music, his father insisted that he study law. Defiantly, Adolphe found music teachers to tutor him in secret.

Eventually, Adolphe proved his ability in composition and the elder Adam relented, but made his son promise that he would avoid writing music for the theater.

Graduated with honors from the Paris Conservatory, he soon established himself as a musician, entertaining the wealthy at parties performing on a harmonium. However, his compositions, which included music for church, piano, and chamber ensembles, lacked distinction.

Abandoning his promise to his father, he tried his hand at grand opera, but without success. He then produced twenty-four

O Holy Night

English translation by John Sullivan Dwight (1813–1893)

Music by Adolphe Charles Adam (1803–1856)
Words by Cappeau de Roquemaure (18??–18??)

comic operettas that were more popular. But it was with ballet that he achieved fame in the European capitals. "Giselle," written in 1841, is a staple in today's ballet repertoire.

Asked by a church in 1847 to produce music for a Christmas Eve midnight mass, Adam wrote a stirring melody, simply called "Cantique de Noël," using as text a poem by his friend Cappeau de Roquemaure. But the church reacted with displeasure and the song was condemned for a "lack of musical taste and total absence of religious spirit."

Fortunately, the public did not agree. "Cantique de Noël" was published and circulated widely, sweeping France and then the world. The co-founder of the Harvard Musical Association, John Sullivan Dwight, translated Roquemaure's poetry into the commonly used English version, "O Holy Night."

Acknowledgments for Christmas Carols

DR. JUNE BASKIN
Christ Episcopal Church, Williamsport, PA
REV. MARK SANTUCCI
Christ Episcopal Church, Williamsport, PA
REV. KEN SAWYER
First Parish Unitarian Church, Wayland, MA
REV. JACK H. HANEY
The Church of the Holy Trinity, Philadelphia, PA
REV. THOMAS D. WINTLE
First Church, Lancaster, MA

Bibliography for Christmas Carol History

Bailey, Albert Edward, *The Gospel In Hymns*. New York: Charles Scribner's Sons, 1950.

Bancroft, Charles, *O Little Town of Bethlehem*. Philadelphia: The Church of the Holy Trinity, 1968.

Barnett, James H., *The American Christmas*. New York: The MacMillan Co., 1954.

Coffin, Tristram Potter, *The Book of Christmas Folklore*. New York: The Seabury Press, 1973.

Cottrell, Leonard, *The Quest for Summer*. New York: G.P. Putnam's Sons, 1965.

Davis, William Stearns, *A Day In Old Rome*. Boston: Allyn and Bacon, 1925.

Dearmer, Percy, R. Vaughan Williams and Martin Shaw, *Oxford Book of Carols*, London: Oxford University Press, 1928.

Duchin, Peter, *A Musical Christmas With Peter Duchin*. New York: Holt, Rinehart and Winston, 1976.

Eckel, Rev. Edward Henry, *Chronicles of Christ Church Parish*. Williamsport, PA: Press of Gazette and Bulletin, 1910.

_____, *Encyclopedia Americana*. Danbury, Connecticut: Grolier, Inc., 1988.

Emurian, Ernest K., *Stories of Christmas Carols*. Boston: W.A. Wilde Co., 1958.

Fowler, W. Wade, *Roman Festivals*. London: MacMillan and Co., Ltd., 1899.

Hadfield, Miles and John, *The Twelve Days of Christmas*. London: Cassell and Co., Ltd., 1961.

Johnston, Harold Whetstone, *Private Life of the Romans*. Chicago: Scott, Foresman, 1903.

Lewis, Taylor, Jr. and Joanne Young, *Christmas In New England*. New York: Holt, Rinehart and Winston, 1972.

Lloyd, Seton, *The Archeology of Mesopotamia*, London: Thames and Hudson, Ltd., 1978.

Lützow, Count, *The Story of Prague*. London: J.M. Dent and Co., 1902.

Poling, Daniel A., *Treasury of Best Loved Hymns*. London: Pickwick Press, 1942.

Protestant Episcopal Church of the U.S.A., *The Hymnal 1940 Companion*, Norwood, MA: The Plimpton Press, 1949.

Samson, William, *A Book of Christmas*. New York: McGraw Hill Book Co., 1968.

Shekerjian, Haig and Regina, *A Book of Christmas Carols*. New York: Harper and Row, 1963.

Simon, William L., Editor, *Reader's Digest Merry Christmas Songbook*. New York: Reader's Digest Association, 1981.

Sweitzer, Elizabeth, editor, *A Collection of Bicentennial Essays* Presented by the First Parish Unitarian Church of Wayland. Wayland, MA: First Parish, 1980.

Thomson, S. Harrison, *Czechoslovakia In European History*. Princeton: Princeton University Press, 1943.

Watts, Franklin, editor, *The Complete Christmas Book*. New York: Franklin Watts, Inc., 1958.

Weiser, Francis X., *The Christmas Book*. New York: Harcourt, Brace and Co., 1952.

Wernecke, Herbert H., *Christmas Songs and Their Stories*. Philadelphia: The Westminster Press, 1957.